The Actor's Business Plan

The Actor's Business Plan

A Career Guide for the Acting Life

JANE DRAKE BRODY

Bloomsbury Methuen Drama
An imprint of Bloomsbury Publishing Plc

B L O O M S B U R Y

LONDON · OXFORD · NEW YORK · NEW DELHI · SYDNEY

Bloomsbury Methuen Drama
An imprint of Bloomsbury Publishing Plc

Imprint previously known as Methuen Drama

50 Bedford Square	1385 Broadway
London	New York
WC1B 3DP	NY 10018
UK	USA

www.bloomsbury.com

BLOOMSBURY, METHUEN DRAMA and the Diana logo are trademarks of Bloomsbury Publishing Plc

First published 2015
Reprinted 2016

British Library Cataloguing-in-Publication Data
A catalogue record for this book is available from the British Library.

ISBN: PB: 978-1-4725-7369-8
ePDF: 978-1-4725-7371-1
ePub: 978-1-4725-7370-4

Library of Congress Cataloging-in-Publication Data
Brody, Jane.
The actor's business plan : a career guide for the acting life / Jane Drake Brody.
pages cm
Includes bibliographical references and index.
ISBN 978-1-4725-7369-8 (paperback)
1. Acting—Vocational guidance. I. Title.
PN2055.B77 2015
792.02'8023—dc23
2015007120

Series: Performance Books

Typeset by RefineCatch Ltd, Bungay, Suffolk
Printed and bound in Great Britain

This book is in honor of absent friends:
Julia Neary, John Dennis, Michael Shurtleff.
I love them still.

Contents

From the Introduction to The Big Funk *by John Patrick Shanley.*

Don't act for money. You'll start to feel dead and bitter.

Don't act for glory. You'll start to feel dead, fat, and fearful.

We live in an era of enormous cynicism. Do not be fooled.

You can't avoid all the pitfalls. There are lies you must tell. But experience the lie. See it as something dead and unconnected that you clutch. And let it go.

Act from the depth of your feeling imagination. Act for celebration, for search, for grieving, for worship, to express that desolate sensation of wandering through the howling wilderness.

Don't worry about Art.

Do these things, and it will be Art.

Preface

I can't avoid beginning this book without a beautiful quote from John Shanley. While it seems odd and silly to advise an actor not to act for money in a book devoted to career planning, Shanley's advice is the only way to maintain a career in a world that has too much money and not enough joy. If you wanted to become rich, you would have gotten a degree in finance, or law, or business. You would have entered those worlds and remained in them. If you did get a degree in such fields because your parents told you to do so, or because you were being "practical," you would not be reading this book. Something in you is calling you to act. Again Shanley in the same essay says:

It's a question of spirit. My ungainly spirit thrashes around inside me making me feel lumpy and sick. My spirit is this moment dissatisfied with the outward life I inhabit. Why does my outward life not reflect the enormity of the miracle of existence?

It is one of the paradoxes of pursuing an art form as a means of earning a living that once one is accomplished enough to enter the performance world, most of one's time is spent doing business of one sort or another. Any working actor or musician will affirm this truth. For many actors this one fact ends promising careers. I remember hearing James Brown, the controversial soul singer, discussing his career. He said something to the effect that he spent 10 percent of his time making music, and 90 percent of his time making it possible to do so.

In my life as an actress, casting director, acting teacher, and director, I have seen many of the most talented and hardworking artists decide to abandon the thing they most love. They lose their way and purpose, they are unable to experience the seeming "lie" of commerce and self-promotion as simply a necessary "lie" that can be discarded as Shanley says in his poem. Many actors view any compromise as an assault on their authenticity—they lack the ability to accept and let it go. They have a problem maintaining the spirit that moves them towards the thing that they were set on the earth to accomplish.

I began my life as an actress, and was never given any advice or instruction about what to do after college. This book is a remedy for the actors that I teach, and for those across the country who have the will but lack an understanding of how to live in a world of such difficulty.

Like many of you, I wanted to be a serious actress doing serious work with great directors, but I was a little girl whose dreams far outdistanced my ability to make any sort of a plan, or even to believe that such a thing was possible. As far as I knew, "professional" meant making money, and I wanted to be a professional, paid actress. I wanted to put that profession on my tax forms. I believed in money.

I went to auditions, and because I was a fairly good singer and a decent actress, I began to be cast in musicals and musical revues. I never made a decision about doing such work, except that I needed to be paid to prove to the world that I was a pro. It was the money that I thought made one legitimate.

This is not unreasonable; I had no financial support, none from my family, and I had started working quite early in my life. After I turned 18, I had to pay my own way while putting myself through school, and therefore doing what I loved to do seemed right somehow. I earned most of my college tuition singing in musical revues in nightclubs.

It never occurred to me that I had to view my career, such as it was, as a business—an artistic one, but a business nonetheless. That is where most of us fail. We drift from show to show with no real focus on where we wish to end up. I never realized that unless I planned my life—life would plan it for me. Luckily, there was one event as a young performer that awakened my need to steer my own life and actually achieve my dreams.

I had been doing a production of *Fiddler on the Roof* in a large dinner theatre in Minneapolis for months, and when the show finally closed a fellow member of the cast, Tom Sherohman, invited me to have lunch with him. Tom was known in the city as a director, performer, stage manager, improviser, and producer. He was a dreamer, with the kind of brain that searches the world for what interests it and proceeds to learn everything there is to know on the subject. He was a bulldog, determined to make art, with no regard for the money to be made. He had faith that the money would follow. This was a philosophy that I had not considered.

Over an omelet, Tom proposed that we do a musical revue he had devised, based on the music of Noel Coward and Cole Porter, at The Brave New Workshop. Why say no? We spent the next six months of 1970 doing the revue entitled *Noel and Cole*, and in turn I became an expert on the two songwriters and on the history of the period from which they emerged. I learned the value of intensive research, as well as a commitment to making an artistic statement, from Tom.

As we performed *Noel and Cole* the Vietnam War was taking its toll on our friends and families. While we were dressing in the basement boiler room (getting very little money), we talked about various things and discovered that during World War II our fathers had both been musicians in the army. We were both radically opposed to the Vietnam War, but we were distressed about one of our generation's mottos: "Never trust anyone over thirty." We admired the people who had fought in World War II and their belief in the righteousness of the cause, as well as the music of that era which supported it.

From these realizations we decided to create a musical revue with the idea of somehow doing our bit to reunite our peers with their parents. Because of the success of *Noel and Cole*, Dudley Riggs, a former circus performer and owner of the theatre, said he would give us some start-up money, and a local theatre critic agreed to help out with additional finances and production advice. Our brilliant pianist, Robert Grusecki (a young music major at the U of M) got on board to arrange the music and accompany. Tom, Bob, and I were the artistic directors and the rest of the *Noel and Cole* cast happily joined in the project we called *Nice Faces of 1943*.

The first artistic and philosophical decision we made was that we would limit the music written between 1941 and 1945. The second was that the music should not be well known to our generation. The third decision was that all of the costumes and props needed to be authentic, and the fourth was that we would somehow link it all together with slides and audiotapes from the period. We gave ourselves artistic parameters. This concept, limiting choices based on artistic and philosophical ideas, became a grounding principle for my future life. As Orson Welles said over lunch one day, "The enemy of art is having no limitations."

There were no computers—slides and audiotapes were cut on cutting boards and assembled by hand. Luckily, my husband was a radio producer and knew how to edit audiotape. And more luck— we lived in a house previously occupied by a rock and roll group who had left abruptly and we inherited their copier! It was a huge thermal printer that must have weighed about thirty-five pounds and used a special kind of paper that was heated to make an impression on it.

Such was our passion that we would dutifully climb the stairs of the Minneapolis Public Library carrying the mammoth thing and slowly copy every piece of pop music in their extensive collection written between December 7, 1941 and August 15, 1945. Other cast members hunted for props; I went from the Salvation Army to the Goodwill to the Veteran's Thrift Shop, and to used-clothing stores all over the city to find the still-available clothes and uniforms of the era.

Everyone contributed to the selection of material and everyone had an opinion. As producing director, Tom had the final say, and though we fought, it was about whether or not a song would help or hinder our mission. Each argument helped us to further define what it was we were trying to say. We were working to structure our production and achieve our goals. Conflict was our friend. We experienced compromise in action.

I was learning how to plan; how to go from a huge idea to the steps needed to make sure the artistic and philosophical dreams became a reality. I was discovering the importance of conflict to the evolution of artistic ideas. There was no ego involved. We were all on the same train and we all listened to nothing but 40s' music during this time. We were experts on the tilt of a hat, dress colors, and the difference in styles in jitterbug dancing. We fell in love with FDR, we did pictures in a World War II bomber near the Veteran's Home. We literally thought ourselves back to the war years. We moved past the idea of dramaturgy as a separate entity, and literally embodied the ideas and images needed for our work.

We finally opened the show, a joy for all of us, and woke up the next morning to reviews in the *Minneapolis Tribune* and in the

St. Paul Pioneer Press that were love letters of deeply-felt praise. They had understood that our mission was to open a dialogue between the generations who were so at odds with each other over the war. The call for generational healing was heard. We had done what we had set out to do, and the money started coming!

We sold out for months. People from all over the country came to see us, many more than once; kids brought their parents. We toured all over the country for about two years with two companies out, always getting rave reviews. Along the way, we were asked to make changes, some good and some bad. But little by little, without noticing it, we had become a vehicle for making money, not for changing the world.

Finally, a producer optioned the show for Broadway. We did a backer's audition at Sardi's in New York, and when we saw our show through the filter of the New York commercial theatre we realized that what the big-time producers wanted from us was far from our original intention. We were forced to grapple with the compromises we would have to make for Broadway. *Nice Faces* would have to be changed from a show concerning the generational conflict over Vietnam to a nostalgia piece, a nice museum piece, but not one of substance.

The war had ended and we had never meant to glamorize World War II. And so, in order to preserve our integrity, we packed up our music, our props, and our costumes, left New York and went our separate ways. I have never regretted that action.

After *Nice Faces*, and several other adventures, I moved to Los Angeles where I studied with the renowned Michael Shurtleff, former casting director and author of *Audition: Everything You Need to Know to Get the Part*. I became his personal assistant, and he became my mentor.

I was extremely successful in LA for the first six months I was there, doing several TV shows as well as a well-received play for which I won an acting award. And then my agent retired. Despite everything I tried for the two years after that, I was unable to get another theatrical agent and my access to film and television was denied. I did have a commercial agent, and was able to support myself doing commercials, but a career acting in film was never anywhere near my grasp.

After trying to fit into various molds, getting my teeth fixed, losing weight, and loads of humiliation, I realized that I was in danger of becoming someone who was far more interested in simply being hired than in the art of acting. It was like the *Nice Faces* experience in New York: my "show" wasn't the one that they wanted. I was losing my soul attempting to please others. I had lost my way. I was looking for ways to make money again. Eventually, I looked up from the swamp of my own negativity and it became obvious that I had to leave LA to save my soul, just as we had left New York.

Looking back I realize that I had moved to LA because I thought that was what actors *should* do. It never occurred to me to question such a move. In reality, I had never wanted to be on TV, in films or commercials. I had not followed my deeper dreams of becoming a stage actress. The only thing that I had done right was to study with Michael Shurtleff who said to me when I announced that I was leaving, "If you stay here for five years, they will want nothing but you." My reply was that if I stayed for five years there would be nothing left of me, though the concept of five years stayed with me. I began to see my life in a series of five-year increments.

Nice Faces gave me the understanding that happiness rests in living your values, in working on things in which you passionately believe, and in knowing when to walk away. It gave me courage to go into the larger world, to believe in my own vision, to understand that money doesn't necessarily mean professionalism, and to know that listening to one's own inner voice is the best way to happiness. I learned the value of commitment, planning, clear goals, and integrity. I brought those ideas to my own career. That career has taken many turns, from singer, to actress, to director, to agent, to casting director, and to teacher, all of which contribute to this book.

Mrs Brody's guide to a happy career and life

1   Support and collaboration with your peers is an essential element of success. Don't go it alone!

2   One needs a dream larger than one's own desire for fame or money to fuel any project over a long period of time.

3   Very little happens without a mentor, someone who knows more than you.

4 Planning, attention to detail, and tedious labor within a framework produces success.

5 It is not about money, but if you follow your impulses, money may come. Be careful when it does.

6 Luck comes when you are working very hard and often when you are expecting something else.

7 Without integrity you will grow sad.

8 It is the work that matters.

Note to Teachers

The biggest complaint of actors graduating from training institutions is that they have not been prepared for the world. This book is intended to alleviate the problem for student actors as well as actors already struggling in the world at large. I have always straddled the worlds of commerce and art myself and believe that it is not only possible, but also necessary in today's world.

I have formulated the exercises contained herein over years of teaching audition techniques and courses covering "the Biz." I can honestly say that these planning structures have eliminated a lot of suffering for many young actors and aided many to realize career dreams in a far healthier way.

For in-class use, I have formatted the book in thirteen chapters to make it possible to assign a chapter or two per week. I find it ideal for there to be some separation in time between the first four assignments, but after that things can move more quickly. When the students complete the assignments for the semester/quarter they should have a career plan. I use that plan as a final project/exam.

There are blank forms available to download for the various tables and lists at **www.janedrakebrody.com**

Introduction

This book uses the same skills that actors are taught in acting classes almost everywhere in the world but turns them to another use. It gives performers a way to plan for success in their own Life Play while acknowledging the chaos into which they leap.

Entrances

As any actor can tell you, the first entrance is probably the biggest hurdle to overcome during a play. You stand backstage, preparing in whatever way you think will help, you hear your cue, your heart falls to your shoes, and somehow you find the courage to cross from the darkness into the light. Once there, the job may still be difficult, absolute certainty can never be assured, but at least the chasm has been leapt over; it is in the past.

In the present, there is the night's performance where, whether you realize it or not, you are supported not only by the script, but also by the planning and rehearsing that you, the director, the designers, and the technical staff have done. The audience is not aware of the time and effort that has been expended to support the actors and the performance. And you, the actor, must not only remember light cues, costume changes, entrances and exits, but also believe deeply and strongly in the imaginary circumstances of the world of the play, and impart that belief to the entire audience.

Becoming a part of an imaginary world

In this book, we will give you the tools to enter the not-so-imaginary world of the profession. The future is always a journey into the unknown, but knowing the territory and choosing which road to take can lead you more frequently to the desired destination than simply holding your breath and wishing.

In preparing for a role, actors are taught to explore the facts, or to use Konstantin Stanislavski's phrase, "the given circumstances", of the play. These include geography, history, manners, fashions, politics, and all the minutiae of everyday life for the characters in the drama. In asking actors to do this sort of investigation, Stanislavski encouraged his students to use the *Magic If*. "If I were in this world what would I need, see, smell, feel, do?" Fully exploring the world of the play from this perspective makes an actor more and more connected personally to the imaginary universe.

You need to apply these same skills to your Life Play. You must become deeply knowledgeable of the given circumstances in the city or market you are entering and of the relationships that you will need to forge. Until you move to that place and embark on a career wherever you are, these are as imaginary as the given circumstances in any play. Such things include an understanding of the people, places, relationships, methods, protocols, and expectations of the markets in which you wish to work. Without such knowledge, you will be entering your acting career like a bad actor who is not prepared for the scene. And, as we all know, this can lead to disaster.

Conflict

It doesn't matter how you get knocked down in life . . . All that matters is that you've got to get up.

BEN AFFLECK

Actors are going to come in conflict with the world, and had better be prepared to deal with it. Luckily, you have learned the skill of accepting and working with conflict in just about every acting class you have ever taken. Do you recall hearing that all plays are about conflict? What did you do about it? If you were paying attention, you were taught to examine the facts of the play, to discover its major and minor character conflicts, as well as the social, political, emotional, and spiritual difficulties faced by the character. You began to make choices based on this research and to engage with the world of the play. Becoming a professional actor means facing conflict and obstacles daily. In order to meet your career head on, you must plan for setbacks, difficult scenes, times of heartbreak, and times of joy. The more you know, the more likely you are to find strategies to help you cope with the emotions of the moment.

If you really think about it, the skills that you have learned in dealing with conflict on the stage can be easily transferred to your own Life Play. Look at it as you would a dramatic text, do the same sort of analysis, and such an approach will lead to choices that can work to solve the problems presented to you by the real world.

At an early rehearsal, the director will usually have discussed who the protagonist and the antagonist of the play are. But if you are a smart actor you will realize that simply because you only have three lines in the second act, your character believes him or herself to be the protagonist of his or her own life. There are no small parts; only small actors. If you are wise, you will understand that all of the humans in the drama, whether they appear in one short scene, or never leave the stage, are seeking to be heroes within the limitations of their own fictional lives, just as we all do. There are no people in life who are not actually fully human, even if they only appear in the third act; your job as an actor of integrity is to bring as much humanity as possible to these small roles. After all, in your own Life Play, you are the star, and everyone else is viewed through that lens.

When you first enter the profession, you will be a walk-on, an extra. No one will see you as a star of any sort. However, while for the theatrical world you may be a flea on its behind, in your own Life Play you must be the protagonist/hero and prepare for the role of professional actor as much as you would for a role on stage. An amateur actor learns the lines, does them, goes to the party, and laughs about how silly his role was. A professional actor cannot afford such foolish behavior either onstage or off. You must do the work of your business as passionately as you prepare for a role. Act "as if" your career is important and real.

By immersing yourself in the facts, the given circumstances, of the play, you begin to personalize and to discover what the dramatic conflict means for your role. Slowly the "character" changes from "she" to "me." You begin to develop actions and tactics to solve the problems presented to you by the author. As this process happens, working deeply and personally, you might begin to feel a certain confidence because you have a plan of attack. While many actors never feel confident per se, the process of rehearsal at least allows them to enter a scene with some little belief that if they do certain things, the gods of the theatre might smile on them.

Most of you have been taught to do intense and sometimes tedious investigative projects in acting classes. These may include writing biographies, lists, or even full research papers; the vocabulary may be different, but the exercise has the same aim—to ignite your imagination and allow you to slip easily and almost unnoticeably into the world of the play and the character. You already have some understanding of how to do this for the character's world. Take what you have learned to do for the stage and do it for your own world and your own Life Play.

Entering a career

Beginning a career is very like making an entrance. To prepare for a career, one must work as rigorously and suffer the same tedium that often accompanies an actor's preparation. A good entrance is propelled by the certainty of what needs to be done both by the actor and the character. Such clarity is even more important in a career, because the world and its challenges keep changing. Have you ever dreamed the actor's nightmare where you forgot your script, or found yourself in a play that you hadn't rehearsed? This nightmare is a reflection of the fears that we all have of being out of control. In the topsy-turvy world of the acting profession, control is not possible, but you can attempt to be ready for the ride.

WARNING # 1: security, risk, benefit

This above all—to thine own self be true,
And it must follow, as the night the day,
Thou canst not then be false to any man.

SHAKESPEARE, *Polonius,* Hamlet, *Act One, Scene Three*

Actors are like surfboarders, riding an ever-changing ocean, hanging on and waiting for the perfect wave to ride and conquer. Just like surfers, actors take risks in exchange for a chance, however slim, to ride the wave for as long as they can. The business world calls this the risk/benefit ratio. How much risk will you take in order to get what kind of benefit? Be very careful that you consider this situation truthfully, for it will be a guiding principle of your life as an actor. What is having an acting career worth to you?

There is no security in the performer's world, so if you are a person who needs lots of it, you may make yourself very unhappy. The *risk* of drowning may outweigh the *benefit* of a great ride. Or there may be too much elapsed time from one great ride to another to make the risk seem worth taking. This does not mean that you shouldn't act; it does mean that you might be happier acting for fun rather than for your life's work.

If, however, security has never been all that important to you, if you need to live a life of passion and creativity over stability, then grab your surfboard. Be very careful, many surfers think they are invincible, and find to their sorrow that the ocean doesn't care about them or their surfboards.

WARNING #2: talent won't matter

I'm a skilled professional actor. Whether or not I've any talent is beside the point.

MICHAEL CAINE

As an actress, acting teacher, director, and casting director for over forty years, I have noticed that when actors give bad performances it is not because they lack talent, but because they believe that their talent should be sufficient. Therefore, they don't *really* prepare. They neglect to take the time to imagine themselves into the world of the play; they don't bother to fully personalize the facts. They don't do the homework that would propel them past the curtain line onto the stage or the film set with the ability to support themselves in the scene. They don't see an audition as a chance to build a career because they think that getting the job at hand is the most vital part of their life. A career takes time and consistently good work. You are never auditioning for a job; you are always creating the kind of reputation that, with any luck, will pay off in the end.

Perhaps because luck plays such a large part in any actor's career, and so many people who appear to be less "talented" seem to be working, many actors become too cynical to work in depth. Perhaps they don't have as much talent as they thought. Or perhaps they are simply arrogant or lazy, and ignore the "boring" practice and research that other actors, musicians, and athletes do daily. Or perhaps it is easier to fail, because one didn't prepare, than to face the fact that even when you tried your hardest, you weren't chosen. At times, through charm or quirk or good looks, the unready actors succeed. But even when they are awarded for such work, they are often haunted by the belief that they have fooled others, that they will be found out in the end, and that the applause or the job offer was just a fluke.

When under-prepared actors fall on their faces, when the flattery and applause isn't forthcoming, the suffering can be overwhelming and many seek to blame others, or hide away in shame at their inability to access the talent they believe they have. While the world has told them that if they believe in their talent all will be well, the reality is that talent is overrated without the skill and drive to back it up. The old adage that you make your own luck can be hard to swallow when you have had a full diet of disappointment.

WARNING #3: waiting or doing

The abuse of talent in acting is lack of preparation. No matter how much talent you may have to draw people's attention, you can never spend enough time with the material. I'm not saying there isn't anything valuable that can happen with a cold reading or raw instinct, that spontaneity isn't a component of what we do. But it isn't enough if you are charging big money. Prepare as much as your life will allow you to prepare.

MICHAEL SHANNON, *Broadway star, TV star in* Boardwalk Empire, *and Academy Award nominee for* Revolutionary Road

The best actors don't pay any attention to talent; they simply and happily do their work. To have a career, take a silent pledge that even if you are talent-free, homely, and blindingly unintelligent, you are willing to do what is needed to get past those deficiencies. I know it sounds negative, but many have found freedom in releasing themselves from having to prove how talented and smart they are. Kurt Naebig, a well-respected career actor in Chicago commented on this saying:

I spent a lot of time trying to prove to others that I was a good actor. If I'd just focused on the work, and the moment, I wouldn't have needed to prove anything. I spent a lot of time trying to think what "they" the casting people wanted. They just wanted me to be truthful and use myself in the work.

The idea that "If you have talent, you will make it" is absurd. The people who "make it" may or may not have talent, but they do have a dedication to their craft, lots of grit, stamina, dogged determination, and a sense of humor about it all. To quote Dame Judi Dench, *"I think you should take your job seriously, but not yourself. That is the best combination."*

The "talented" actors, who sit on shore, looking out at the sea, or waiting for the phone to ring, while others surf and sail, are waiting for some sort of lucky chance to fall their way. Like Blanche DuBois in *A Streetcar Named Desire*, they want to depend on the "kindness of strangers." This approach to a life and career is guaranteed to create far more chaos and depression than a life where unearned kindness is not expected, where luck is earned through hard work, deep thought, and planning. When luck comes, one needs to be ready to build on it.

Cooling your jets

Now that I have frightened you, I offer you this book as a way of calming the fear and panic of the seemingly impenetrable wall of "the business." As with any performance, preparation and support can help you over the curtain line and onto the stage. In your Life Play, you must put one foot in front of another, connect with your partners, and hope that the show goes well. At that time, everything is beyond your control, your talent has very little to do with it, and the rest is up to the ancient gods of the theatre, Thespis and Dionysius, and the patron saint of actors, comedians, and clowns, Saint Genesius.

1

Dreams for Your Life Play

An acting career is not a job. Many people want to claim that it is, but that is a very reductive way of looking at it. Unlike a job, a career (of any kind) is a life activity that doesn't end after eight hours of labor, nor is it something that you can set aside to get on with your private life. No one suffers so much for a mere job, or is willing to work so cheaply, or to give up so much for a paycheck. I have always considered acting more of a "calling," like the priesthood, than a way of making a living. Acting is a career based in passion and dreams, not in practicalities.

Such passions drive actors to pursue BIG dreams. They spend many thousands of dollars on university training, classes, pictures, résumés, clothes, dental work, and anything else that will give them the ability to make a living doing the thing they most love—acting. They often sacrifice the ordinary things that their peers take for granted: family, stable incomes, home ownership, and leisure activities. And yet, paradoxically, most actors prepare more thoroughly for a scene in an acting class than for their lives. They have no plan of attack, no actual concept of how they will survive beyond the present moment.

If you consider that you are doing the Play of your Life, not planning how the second and third acts will be handled can lead to disaster. However, your acting training has given you an advantage that you may not even realize. You have been taught to analyze a role and to do the things needed to get the play done within the role. In other words, you know how to make a plan that helps you move through the play.

Stanislavski, the man who wrote the bible of acting (recently re-translated and re-formulated as *An Actor's Work* by Jean Benedetti)[1] suggested that actors, when attempting to move into a role, examine the facts of the play to discover what the character most wants or needs. When the need arising from these facts is discovered, it should provoke the character to action, and as the actions add up, the play will be accomplished. He entitled this need the "super-objective or super-task." I have come to believe that this term refers to the actor's decision about the overall action that the character needs to do to achieve their dreams. The reason behind the uninspiring language has to do with Stanislavski's need to please the censors in Stalin's Russia, in order to keep himself, his family and colleagues, and his theatre, alive.

When I was a student actor, "super-objective" sounded like a word used to describe the invasion of another country, a military word; "super-task" seemed like spring-cleaning a house. The words "goals", "tasks", and "tactics" never caught my imagination. They seemed more suited to a corporate boardroom than to a play. I understood them, but it was difficult to find the passion hidden therein. I struggled with finding super-objectives and tasks until I read Michael Shurtleff's classic book *Audition*[2] that uses the word "dream" instead. The idea of the character's *dream* excited me and released me to my imagination. I could understand dreams; they bore a resemblance to my own passionate longings to be an actor. In the play, the essential desire has to be big enough and strong enough to allow the character to do extraordinary things, things of such importance that they would be worthy of an audience. I myself wanted to do an extraordinary thing. I wanted to act.

Doing your Life Play requires big dreams. While many may not be aware of it, in our everyday lives we are motivated by dreams of success, fantasies of having a perfect life. The bigger our dreams, the harder we strive. Plays are about people caught up in great difficulties that force them to do unusual things to achieve their dreams. The

---

[1] Stanislavsky, Konstantin and Jean Benedetti. 2008. *An Actor's Work: A Student's Diary.* London: Routledge.
[2] Shurtleff, Michael. 1978. *Audition, Everything an Actor Needs to Know to Get the Part.* New York: Walker & Company, Bantam.

language of goals and objectives is better used to sell real estate or to manage a factory; these problems are rarely the stuff of the theatre. So, in the planning documents in this book, we will not use corporate terms, we will use the tools we have been given as actors—imagination, passion, the ability to look at a scene from different viewpoints, rehearsing until we get it right and hopefully, a sense of humor.

You will be looking not only at your career dreams, but also, and perhaps just as importantly, at your personal life dreams. The two things are inseparable. The timing of a life dedicated to acting doesn't always line up with the desire to have a family, or to travel, or to get another degree, or to do all of the things that less driven people get to do. Finding a balance of any kind between a private life and a professional life can be so difficult that, sadly, one or the other is abandoned. If acting doesn't fulfill you, the sacrifices can be overwhelming. An acting career is like having two loves, the theatre, and the person to whom you are wed.

Right now your job is only to contemplate your dreams, however fantastical. Dream big and be honest! Big dreams such as becoming a member of a prestigious performing company, or appearing as a lead on Broadway, or having your own television show, are admittedly difficult to achieve, but other people have done so, and therefore they are within your grasp.

Imagine that you can, and will, win. Michael Shurtleff gave the advice to actors in a love scene that they should always believe that their partner is actually in love with them but is too silly to realize it. The action then is to awaken them to that happy fact rather than to fight to make the partner love them. If you get behind the idea that what you have to offer is a gift to the world, however modest, you may find yourself in the position to give it. However, if you view the world as needing to give _you_ something, you will remain a beggar, pleading for the world to love you.

After you investigate your dreams in this chapter, in the following chapters you will go on to examine the given circumstances in which the obstacles to them lie. You will determine actions that can make your life move forward to achieve a happy ending for your Life Play. In looking at these ideas, you will be identifying your values and your motivations. These will support you through the difficulties thrown at you by the given circumstances. A plan built on dreams is far more substantial than one built on goals.

Section one: committing your dreams to writing

Dreaming, after all, is a form of planning.

GLORIA STEINEM

Your first assignment in this book is to envision at least six or more dreams concerning your career as an artist. Commit them to paper and avoid editing. Aim high and be as specific as possible! Having a specific vision will make your path clearer. Okay! Go! Make the first list!

Example: artistic dreams

1 To appear as a regular on *Saturday Night Live*.

2 To be directed by Peter Brook.

3 To do *Macbeth* in New York.

4 To create work with underprivileged children and make the world better.

5 To write and produce my own films.

6 To win an Oscar, or a Tony, or both, for best actor.

7 To found a theatre with a group of likeminded actors in my home town.

8 To do a solo performance based on the life of Bette Davis.

Artistic dreams: questions to ponder

People will kill you over time,
And how they'll kill you
Is with tiny, harmless phrases,
Like "be realistic."

DYLAN MORAN, *Irish comedian, actor, writer*

Open your secret heart and don't worry about appearing silly. Dreams are fantasies, not realities. You are allowed to think selfishly. Don't be ashamed of your dreams. Open your mind to them and consider that people with just as much self-doubt, lack of self-love, and low self-esteem have careers on stage and on screen. There is no requirement to consider obstacles or practicalities right now.

If there were no obstacles, where would you want to be in five years? Be specific and maybe do some research. Regional theatres such as the Tyrone Guthrie in Minneapolis, the Actors Theatre of Louisville, and the American Repertory Theater in San Francisco are different from theatres that are generally dedicated to musicals. Musical theatres are not limited to Broadway; they include such theatres as the Drury Lane in Chicago, the Zach in Austin, Texas, and the Chanhassen in Minnesota. Do you want to venture forth and start your own company like Steppenwolf in Chicago or The Woolly Mammoth in Washington DC, or the Ensemble Theatre in Cincinnati, or the Depot Theater in Dodge, Kansas?

Do you want to be a working actor who doesn't deal with the problems of fame? One who lives in a small market and works all the time? Where? Do you want to be a recognized "star" in films or TV? What kind? What directors do you want to work with? Do you long to become a regular in a sitcom? Do you even know what these things are?

Many actors say, "I just want to work." An admirable desire, but it doesn't generate enough heat to make a lifetime career. In the final analysis, such a viewpoint leaves you aiming at every target and missing most of them. Stanislavski said, "The general is the death of art." He meant that we don't live our lives generally; we live them specifically, and therefore the actor must investigate the specifics of the play. The same is true of anyone working on their Life Play. It is not enough for me to say that I want to be in show business and live in the United States; there is not enough information in that statement to be helpful. If I say I want to live in Chicago and do theatre there, that is still rather vague, but if I say that I want to live on the North Side, between Andersonville and Lincoln Square, and work as an actress at Second City, you might, with some research, be able to make some inferences about my life and me. The more information you can give, the clearer the picture becomes.

Is your dream to do Shakespeare? Be specific! Where? Shakespearean theatres exist all over the country, and each one has a different personality. They include the Chicago Shakespeare Theater, the Ashland Shakespeare Festival, the Shakespeare Company in DC, the Atlanta Shakespeare Company, Shakespeare in the Park in New York, the Utah Shakespeare Festival and many others, large and small.

In the same way, if you said that you wanted to work in Los Angeles, you have said very little. If you say that you want to work in comedy in Los Angeles, that will help, and if you say you want to do an improvisational comedy show on an alternative network with a company of actors, such a statement will finally give the world (and you) some real information.

Section two: real life dreams

Acting is everybody's second job.

JACK NICHOLSON

The one place where most actors fail in their careers is not in their careers. It is in admitting to themselves that as full human beings they will eventually want the normal things everyone else wants from life. This book encourages you to look at ALL of your life dreams. Commit to them and write them down. Make a list of six or more ideas in each category (artistic, personal, money, day job, education, service). Remember, these are dreams! Later you can sort out how these things might happen; again, don't be realistic, realism will come later.

All of us want and need some sort of financial security, we all want loving relationships, we all want to spend our days pleasantly, we all want to continue to grow, and we all want to think of ourselves as good people. Failure to consider these personal needs is the number one reason that actors abandon their careers.

Frequently, the problem comes down to impatience exacerbated by financial need brought about by embarking on a career journey with no real destination or timetable in sight. Without a map, or a metaphoric place to which one wants to go, there is no reason to assume a successful journey. Why do talented and intelligent people leave home without GPS? I suspect it has to do with the fear of confronting actualities. Actors, like many others, don't really like to look such things directly in the face. They want to depend on fate. Think for a minute what fate does to those who don't want to face the truth: Oedipus, or King Lear, or Walter White. Not a good idea.

Reasons given by those who have left the business

- "I hated waiting tables, it felt so demeaning and I didn't like working with the customers. I quit and got a day job where I didn't have to sweat for tips."

- "I wanted to have children, and so, I postponed my career until after my family was raised."

- "I grew really tired of not getting cast. I spent an awful lot of time and energy wishing for jobs—time and energy I should have used to be better prepared for auditions (reading more plays, seeing plays despite my jealousy, knowing my audition material cold). And I eventually felt bitter and resentful. I didn't want to risk being rejected again, so I sabotaged myself by not being as prepared as I could be or by doing something that would communicate, 'F-you I don't want your stupid job anyway.' "

- "I hated the business, the constant disappointment, the feeling that no one wanted me, and I didn't want to do the agent and casting director thing anymore."

- "I discovered that I was neither pretty enough nor talented enough."

- "I fell into the semi-professional dinner theatre circuit and decided that making money that way wasn't worth the effort."

- "I had so much student debt that I couldn't see my way through to quitting my day job."

- "I just didn't like living in New York!"

In order to avoid such problems, I strongly suggest, beg, and implore you to take the Myers-Briggs Test (MBT). The test may be freely administered by your university, or you may want to pay the actual Myers-Briggs organization to take it by going to their website (**www. myersbriggs.org**). There are other similar sites available free online, and I like this one—**www.humanmetrics.com**—but there are many others listed at **www.123test.com**. I am not implying that a test of this sort is a 100 percent predictable method of trait assessments; however it is a means to start a conversation with yourself about yourself!

My MBT profile says that I am an "ENFJ." Such a profile indicates the ways in which you prefer to interact with the world. (When you take the test, the terms are explained in an easy to understand manner.) My results from the Myers-Briggs test are given in the list below. The "judging and perceiving" item is a "judgment" call.

- You have a clear preference of extraversion over introversion.

- You have a very clear preference of intuition over sensing.

- You have a slight preference of feeling over thinking.

- You have a preference of perceiving over judging, but that is modified by many of your other answers.

Here are some possible career paths for an "ENFJ" (from the **humanmetrics.com** website).

- Facilitator.

- Consultant.

- Psychologist.

- Social worker/counselor.

- Teacher.

- Clergy.

- Sales representative.

- Human resources.

- Manager.

- Events coordinator.

- Politician/diplomat.

- Writer.

Looking at my list I find that it is amazingly true for me. I have been a consultant and a *facilitator*, which is a major part of being a casting director. And, of course, casting is all about *human resources*! I read heavily in psychology and need to understand it as a teacher of actors. A part of my teaching job is *counseling* young actors. *Clergy* seems reasonable because I am concerned with spiritual things. Before I began teaching and casting I was a *sales representative* for a cosmetics company and was asked to become a *manager* for the product. I am *politically active*, even though I don't think I would be a very good diplomat (too straightforward for that). As a director, I certainly *coordinate events*, and, it may seem obvious, but as of now, I am a *writer*.

This test, like many others can be wrong, but I have found that in general people who take it seem to agree that it is fairly accurate. Print out what the test says to you and ponder it. Keep it near you as you work on your day job dreams. Look at the interpretations and suggestions on the website and note them. Once you have examined your results, you can go on to start your first five-year life a bit more easily!

Categories of real-life dreams

- Day jobs: non-theatre work.

- Money.

- Family and friends.

- Education and self-improvement.

- Service to the world.

Day jobs

Recently, someone looking at my plan to include day job happiness in this book said that doing so was not a good idea. He postulated that if actors were happy in their day jobs, they would therefore not continue to act. In other words, he was saying that actors must have jobs they only tolerate until such time as they "make it" in the biz. This seems just plain stupid to me. Actors want to act, and paychecks don't stop that desire. If a day job becomes more attractive than acting, the actor in question may not have the kind of passion needed to suffer the slings and arrows of a career. Happiness is the most important thing we can get from life and it doesn't really matter from whence happiness comes.

However, actors are squeamish about considering day jobs other than as necessary things they must do to earn a subsistence living while waiting for a break. They shy away from investigating ways in which these jobs might help them to live a fuller life. I think that having a day job that offers a feeling of accomplishment or appreciation can only result in an actor who isn't desperate. Desperation is impossible to bear and it wreaks havoc on an artist. We have all heard the phrase, "Never let them see you sweat," and it is a great piece of advice. If you are too needy, you become a beggar, wanting someone to give you something, and that is never an attractive thing to bring to an audition. Los Angeles agent, Liz Hanley, of BiCoastal Talent says, "Find something that gives you bliss besides being on stage or in front of the camera. In your bliss, comes your success!" Please! Don't back away from this category; it is vital to your ability to maintain yourself as a beginning actor.

Day job dreams

1   Work in a bookstore or a library.

2   Teach sailing and take people on cruises.

3   Become a private chef.

4   Do carpentry.

5   Work for a charitable foundation.

6   Own an organic farm.

Pondering a day job

I often ask actors I am counseling the following question, "If there were no theatres, films, TV shows or other entertainment outlets, what would you be happy doing?" Most of them stutter and stammer, protest the idea, and begrudgingly come up with one or two very pale ideas. However, this is the best question to ask yourself in order to stimulate some creative thinking.

Actors lead varied lives and rarely rely completely on the income derived from their artistic work. You will seldom have any control over when and where you will be employed. After a while, this insecurity can create such an emotional and financial toll that you will be forced to drop out. When I was casting full time (before computers) I had filing cabinets of pictures separated by age and gender. The categories were children, teens, 20–25, 25–30, 30–40, 40–50, 50–60, 60–80. There were at least eight drawers containing 20–25, five for 25–30, three for 30–40, and one each for the remaining ages. My conclusion is that by the time actors are 30, the majority of them have left the market. Some have moved to LA or NYC, but most have given up.

Artists who have a "day job" that they enjoy, one that gives them control over their lives, are far happier and have longer artistic lives. And, oddly enough, a day job may inform your acting career in ways that you would never foresee.

For an artist the best kind of day job is one that he or she has created. Actors who become small-business people using their life skills tend to be the happiest. Many of my students paint houses, have dog-walking services, cater weddings and other events, create websites for others, write grants, or clean and repair apartments for owners when a tenant leaves. There are as many job niches as there are skills and needs. Be creative—if you are good at something, chances are there is a way to make a living doing it. From an anonymous actor: "I have had an online business selling vintage records for about six years. A third to half of my income comes from it now. Did it coz it was a hobby and it paid off."

There are also positions in the business world that can offer scheduling flexibility, and the ability to set your own hours, or create your own weekly schedule. These jobs assist you in withstanding the unpredictable nature of the business. "Temp" agencies that provide employers with temporary employees can be of great help in this instance. Many such agencies are happy to work with performers because actors' skills include: taking direction, working on a schedule, good verbal and communication skills, working with a team, and generally strong clerical, research, and writing skills. Temp agencies can provide you with the days or weeks of employment you need, and it is not unusual to be offered full-time employment by the company where you have been "temping."

When that happens, the ball is in your court. You have some negotiating power; you are able to ask for what you need in the job. "I am an actor, and may have auditions or bookings during the day. I will make sure that I get the job done, but I need flexibility. If that is all right with you I would love to accept your offer." If this seems far-fetched to you, I have known many actors who have been able to do this, and their employers have been supportive and excited to have such a person on their staff. If the employer says "no," there is always another temp job!

> I work the front desk at a downtown hotel—eight-hour shifts. They're really good about letting me switch around my schedule if an audition or a rehearsal pops up. Since it's a hotel, it has to be open twenty-four hours, and there's always another shift I can switch to if I have to give one up. Also, I just got lucky with really easy-going managers.
>
> SAM HAINES, actor at the beginning of his career

In New York, actress Barbara Poole gives the following advice:

> I was working part-time in the travel department for a student-exchange service in NYC. I negotiated a flex-time schedule with my employer by 1) doing EXCELLENT work; 2) discussing my time needs honestly with my manager; and 3) presenting a well-thought-out plan to allow me to shift from salary to hourly which my boss then only had to sign off on. (An alternate scenario would be to present a plan then negotiate acceptable changes from management.) And, most importantly, aside from Item 1, 4) be willing to walk away. If you're truly an excellent employee, an employer would much rather accommodate than replace.

You do need to be resourceful in looking for jobs. There are so many ways of making a living but most of us theatre people rarely pay any attention to them. We don't actually know what it is that people in the real world do! One of my former students, Kristy Staky, learned to make wigs as a part of her class in theatrical make-up and she got good at it. She now has a business in LA called "Top Knot" and she makes her living creating wigs while pursuing an acting career. Another student, a wonderful Chicago actor, Stephen Rose, has a well-paid job in the e-learning development business. He writes:

Most of these jobs will be for between three and six months. There are agencies, much like talent agencies that parse out the jobs. Pay for e-learning development can run as high as $120 an hour. Take some graphic design or instructional design courses while you are at school, and you can make your own schedule. I think it's the perfect job for someone to get some experience before they leave school and get some quick temp jobs by applying at a lower salary, $20 per hour, until they get a "reputation" for good work. The other trend in corporate training is towards video. Being able to write, produce and direct ten-minute training videos is currently the hottest thing in corporate training. Lots of similarities and crossover skills. Again, a class in instructional design (basically Harold Clurman directing theory in reverse) would be needed on a résumé. But I bet you could make a nice living on three video projects a year and have a lot of free schedule outside of project deadlines.

And I couldn't leave this out from an actor who is well-trained in improvisation (his company is called Innovise Guys):

We use improvisation, fused with CPS (creative problem solving/ brainstorming) to do innovation work with Fortune 500 clients and non-profits to create new products, team-build, manage change, process improvement, train/teach, etc. We have directly created new products, have sparked seven-plus patents, presented/ work-shopped internationally.

When I was living in LA, I stumbled into a great day job. I answered an ad seeking people who had experience with make-up for a flexible full- or part-time job. It was for Prescriptives Cosmetics and I became what is known as a "product" or "field representative." My job, which paid very well and allowed me to make my own schedule, was to go to department stores and teach salespeople how to sell the products, to occasionally do makeovers in the aisles, and to represent the brand to the customers in whatever store I was visiting. I was offered the job because, as a theatre student, I was trained in make-up, and as an actress, I was skilled in interpersonal communication by the very nature of my training. I was not afraid of having an audience, whether it was three shoppers debating skin care solutions at the counter, or a team of saleswomen in a training room. This was a role I easily played; I had been trained to do it. And in looking at my Myers-Briggs profile, I was doing a job that the test suggested I would be good at (consultant, psychologist, teacher, sales representative).

I have worked as a personal assistant doing grocery shopping and other such mundane tasks for a businesswoman, I did some investigative shopping (that is fun), and I worked taking inventory at various stores during their end of year assessments.

Many actors are "standardized patients." These actors pretend (improvise) to have various diseases for doctors in training. They assess the doctor's bedside manner and his or her diagnostic skill. The job pays well and the actors get to do what they love to do!

Before doing the cosmetics lady gig, I was waiter. I loved it. For me it was like doing a show every night; I loved meeting people, I loved the challenge of balancing my tables, and getting the food out on time. I found it very pleasurable to make sure that everyone was happy and, when I was at the restaurant, my time flew by without me even noticing. Needless to say, the money was good. However, a word to the wise—if you are waiting tables, working at a diner is not the best idea. Go where the money is because that is were the tips are best. I am not saying don't wait tables. I am saying do something that you like to do, in a place you like to work, and in a skill that you could use even if your career failed.

I have spent so much time discussing day jobs because your happiness depends on your ability to pay your bills and feel that you are valuable in some way. If you decide to do a job that you hate, you will become bitter and angry before you ever have a shot at a career. Remember this is your Life Play, not your life sentence.

Dreams: debt freedom and finances—five years

Paying off student loans and planning for the future

You will want to do this in order to (for example):

1 Be free and clear of credit card and student loan debt.

2 Be able to support my disabled sibling.

3 Be able to live without a day job.

4 Own my own home/condo.

5 Be able to travel and study.

6 Be able to give money to people less fortunate than myself.

7 Buy a house for my grandmother.

Pondering financial dreams: five years

Money equals freedom to choose, it is as simple as that. Without sufficient funds, you will feel trapped and frustrated. Unless you are one of the lucky people who can live on trust funds or inheritances, getting money will be the uppermost thought in your mind much of the time. While you are in school, it may seem as if that won't be a problem for you, but when you graduate you will see things quite differently.

Most artists aren't motivated by money, and the fantasy of making a million dollars doesn't actually excite us. We want to be able to live simply but without financial strain. That is not the same as needing to make tons of bucks! Be very honest with yourself here. If you truly want to make a six-figure income and know that such a thing is important to you, than go ahead and put it down as a dream, but don't just write, "I want to be a millionaire" if you don't actually need to be that.

One of the most helpful questions to ponder is "How much do you think a person five years older than you are now should be making?" This figure can help you see beyond the fashionable idea that becoming wealthy is the most important thing in life.

Dreams: personal relationships and family

Personal dreams

1 To be married or live with my life partner.

2 To have children.

3 To make peace with my family and to be available to them.

4 To keep the friends I have and make new ones.

5 To be the person who takes care of my friends in times of need.

6 To be a home away from home for my siblings.

Pondering personal dreams and family

We all need love. People who say they don't are fooling themselves. We may not all admit that we want romantic love, but really, we do. It seems to be biological. Humans live and work in pairs and in tribes. These connections allow us to venture forth with the knowledge that there is in this world a place where we are welcomed and valued. Finding such love is a difficult thing and preoccupies our minds until we either get it or give up on it. Giving up on it doesn't generally happen until we are in our late 40s. We need support. Maintaining loving relationships is probably the biggest challenge of our lives, bigger than money and bigger than careers. The young actor quoted below has already faced the problem once:

> *For a year, I wound up in a romantic relationship that wasn't supportive of my career. My focus got split. And I felt myself neglecting opportunities and underpreparing. Then I ended the relationship. It was right at that point (no joke) that real things started happening for me . . . because I was dedicating myself to my craft 100 percent.*
>
> COLIN SPAHR, actor, Chicago

For the following actor, the problem is viewed differently:

I chose to be an actor, and I tour with musicals a lot of the time. I do see it as giving up a home life to tour—I choose to tour. I don't see it as giving up my relationship to be on location—I maintain my relationship however I can do so while doing my job.

D. C. ANDERSON, actor, New York City

For actors, having children is very difficult, but it is a dream for many people, both men and women. If you truly want children and have always wanted them, put them in the dream column. But be aware what the dream actually is. Are you dreaming of having children because you need your parent's approbation? Are you doing so because it is expected of you? For many of us, children are not something we actually crave. If that is true for you, don't feel selfish or ashamed or a disappointment to your parents. There are more than enough children in the world, and you don't have to reproduce to please anyone:

I feel like I have a good balance—but mostly because I have wholeheartedly decided not to have kids. To me, my creative pursuits are most important.

SUZI BARRETT, actress, TV, film, improvisation, Los Angeles

And from Kurt Naebig, an actor, director, and teacher from Chicago:

Finding balance has been difficult. Always a work in progress, but I have friends, I have kept my family intact, I have two daughters, a home, insurance, a 401K, some downtime, vacations, and a career that I would not give up for anything. I love this business and the excitement of a career that changes every day.

Finally, from an older actor looking at what he has found to be true over the years:

In the beginning there was nothing, nothing, nothing more important to me than the theatre. Romantic relationships suffered, family obligations were ignored, etc.—there was no balance at all. I'm older now, and I think that's a huge part of it. I became a father and that definitely has been a huge part of it. Now my son is #1; if

I had to give all this up for him I would, gladly. And I have also realized more fully the value of long-term relationships, friendships, and a balance between theatrical obligations and more personal obligations. The truth is, all this balance makes you a better human, and being a better human makes you a better actor.

JEFF STILL, NYC-based actor, New York

Many actors choose to have children but rely on very supportive mates as well as close friends and family to help with the inevitable chores of raising happy and healthy kids. It can be done, and having such an extended network of caretakers might actually be in your dream:

I have a 2-year-old and another on the way. We live in a large house in Hyde Park with two other families and a couple of single people. We share meals and expenses. It is wonderful. Because we are willing to live like this, we have been able to save money and worry less. I would advise all young artists to Google "intentional communities." It's like having roommates but there is a system that provides a safe and conflict-free way to share resources.

DUSTIN WHITEHEAD, actor, filmmaker, Chicago

A network of friends tends to be far more important to actors than to other people, and most friends are other theatre people. Theatre people work odd hours, in groups, in short and intense periods of time, all moving towards the same goals. Whether we like each other or not, we understand each other, and we meet again and again throughout our lives because the acting world is so small. For us there is usually only a third degree of separation. Other theatre people keep us sane when the rest of the world finds us insane.

Dreams: education and self-improvement

If you aren't going forward, you are going backward.

Education dreams

1   Study with Austin Pendleton or some other great acting teacher.

2 Learn viewpoints or Suzuki or more Meisner or more
   Shakespeare or SuperScenes.

3 Study on-camera techniques.

4 Become the singer I know I can be.

5 Take dance lessons.

6 Make myself as physically healthy as possible.

Pondering education dreams

It is vital that actors continue to train outside of school; it is very easy
to become rusty and complacent. Just because you graduated with an
acting degree doesn't mean that you are done. You never stop learning
to act; it is an art form that can never be perfected. Even if you want
to do nothing but act in film in LA, always being in an acting class
keeps you alive and ready. You really don't want a big audition to come
your way when all you have been doing for the past year is working
your day job. Liz Hanley, of BiCoastal Talent, LA suggests, "Stay in
audition classes, you can often go weeks without an audition and then
one comes and the actor always says, 'It's been so long, I felt rusty.' "

Make sure that the training you seek is of substance. It should
ADD to your skills and your experience. There are lots of teachers out
there, and as with anything only 10 percent of them are any good. I
have seen actors trapped by this guru or that, who makes them feel
wonderful or beats them to an emotional pulp, but who actually does
little to move the actor from point A to point B. Do your homework
and find out who the top-notch teachers are. If your dream is to study
with the greatest teacher in the world, you can do so. Remember this
list is for your dreams, not your obstacles. There is a list of suggested
non-academic training schools and teachers throughout the US at the
back of this book.

Think outside of the box. If you aren't a dancer, taking a class will
open up new roads of expression for you and add to your castability.
Take voice classes to become a better singer. Take vocal production
lessons to be able to have the best sound you can, to have a voice
capable of expressing every nuance of meaning and emotion, and
perhaps to rid you of regionalisms. It is also very wise to take lots of
audition courses for all media. Many of you were not fortunate

enough to have on-camera work, or as much voice and movement training as you need to be a professional. Create your own graduate program, take classes that challenge you and that help you to get where you want to be, while keeping you artistically fulfilled.

Do you dream of radiating health and beauty? As we all know, stamina and good health are absolutely necessary for actors. The hours we work in rehearsal and the things we are asked to do vocally and physically in a play require centeredness, strength, grace, and the ability to repeat and repeat and repeat. We don't all need to be slender and lithe, but we all need to be physically capable of moving and speaking with ease and purpose. Be sure that you remain true to your own dreams, not those of others, nor what the market expects of you. You will get lots of pressure from agents and managers to fix your nose, or to lose weight, or to gain weight, or to have breast implants, or to develop six-pack abs. This advice may be right or it may be wrong—you need to determine how far you are willing to change yourself to adhere to someone else's standards. This problem is particularly acute for women, but remember Barbra Streisand never got her nose fixed and Brooke Eliott (*Drop Dead Diva*) never lost her weight. Despite these things, both have had very successful careers.

Community service dreams

Actors need to remember that while they may live in the theatre world, the rest of the world (civilians), don't. And generally, films and plays are written about "civilian" problems and challenges, not ours. We lead privileged and sheltered lives and crawling out of our little theatre pods is essential to keeping our feet on the ground. Find ways to make a difference. Such service can put your life into perspective, and that is a valuable thing. Service is not meant to help you figure yourself out though; it is simply the right thing to do for the world.

Community service dreams

1   To work with disabled children.

2   To make a difference in the lives of the elderly.

3 To rescue animals.

4 To work to change the country politically.

5 To reach out to the homeless.

6 To help provide vision to high-school students who have given up.

Pondering community service dreams

People who go into the arts are usually those whose hearts are tender, and who want justice and mercy for the world. Because the pursuit of an acting career is such an enormously difficult and discouraging road to take, actors can easily become completely self-involved without ever recognizing that they have abandoned dreams of helping the world. They focus on helping themselves. The formerly passionate crusader for social justice can easily become a narcissistic being whose only care is about a reputation, a next job, an agent, a nose job, a haircut, great reviews, and who said what to whom about *them*. Where, oh where, did that wonderful young person go? Actors such as Brad Pitt, Michael J. Fox, Susan Sarandon, Morgan Freeman, Matt Damon, Eva Longoria, and many others have made a real difference in the world. And they did it because they felt it was their moral and ethical duty to do so.

Helping others is really a matter of giving time to them. It doesn't take money, or great skill. It takes a willingness to give an hour or four or eight to something outside of yourself. Luckily, young actors often have lots of time, so instead of spending a few hours at the bar, you might decide to spend them on the playground, or in the schoolroom, or in an old-age home, or in a campaign office. Whatever it is, such work will make you feel as if you are accomplishing something, however small, in the world, and that feeling is not easy to obtain for actors at the beginning of their careers.

2

Given Circumstances of Your Life Play:

Obstacles

Now that you have examined your dreams and set them down in their neat categories, it is time to look at the given circumstances—i.e. the facts of your Life Play. The obstacles to achieving your dreams are contained in them, but may not be obvious at first glance. Examine your dream lists, keep in mind your personal circumstances, and quickly decide what obvious obstacles present themselves. Do this very generally. Give it a quick once-over. You will look at these obstacles more specifically in the following chapters, but now, take a few guesses and don't get tied up in knots of negativity.

It is easiest to do this in the same way you first did your dream lists. I am giving you an example of obstacles to artistic dreams, but you should do this for *each category* for which you have established dreams. Okay! Have fun!

Table 2.1 Example of dreams and obstacles

Artistic dream	Obstacles
To appear as a regular on *Saturday Night Live*	Most of those people come from Second City or the Groundlings or something like that. I have never trained in improvisation, and don't know anyone who does it.
To be directed by Declan Donnellan	Declan Donnellan mostly lives and directs in England and in Russia. He also works with his own ensemble and the odds of me getting into that are way high.
To do *Macbeth* in New York	I live in Chicago and am not a name actor. Plus, I haven't done that much Shakespeare even though I love it.
To have my own sitcom	I live in Oklahoma and there is not an industry here. Also, I am not gorgeous like the people I see on TV.
To write and produce my own films	I have only tried to write a script for my writing class and don't understand how screenplays get done. I have no contacts, and the whole thing seems overwhelming.
To win an Oscar, or a Tony, or both	To win any major awards, you have to be in major projects. I am a tadpole in a pond of big bullfrogs, and even if I have the talent, they are able to croak more loudly and have stronger bodies.
To work with the Coen brothers	I have no idea how to reach them, nor what I would do if I did reach them.
To be so sought after that I don't need to audition, just accept scripts	This idea implies that I have made a big success and that I know lots of people in the business. I don't.

3

Your Life Play's
Five-year Plan:

Objectives, Events, Tactics, Beats, and Tasks

By this time, you should have a list for each category with obstacles attached. Now you can break these seemingly enormous dreams and obstacles down into "bits," as Stanislavski would call it.[3] Regardless of how you say it, breaking down a scene or a play into bits, or *beats,* as we call them in the US, is a way of separating the events or happenings into smaller units so that the shape of the play begins to emerge. Once the progression of the beats is determined, the actor's job is to make sure that they occur through their choice of actions. I am ahead of myself in discussing actions at this moment, but we will come to them when the time is right.

The first and most important way to separate your big ideas into smaller and more manageable 'bits' is to separate the potential events of your life by years into a five-year calendar. These five years are the five acts of your first Life Play. They are, of course, projections into the future. After all, that is what dreams are!

---

[3] As Stanislavski says (this is not a direct quote), "We cannot eat an entire turkey without carving it up into bits (beats). And as with turkey, we must cut the big pieces first, the legs, the wings, the thighs, and so forth. After that these pieces must be made smaller so that we can actually eat them. And, having a bit of gravy helps as well."

Making a five-year plan is a practice that small-business people have been doing for many years. The reason for this is that research into success rates for businesses across the country indicates that most small businesses fail within eighteen months, most don't turn a profit until their third year and, if they last that long, successful ones can generally support themselves in five years. The federal government gives you five years to deduct expenses and generate some income before your business is called a hobby.[4] Survival into the fifth year is a good indication that a business, with sufficient attention, will be prosperous for a long time to come.

Young actors often fail because they don't foresee a long climb to success for *themselves*. They secretly think that *others* will have to plan and work and wait, but that *they*, because they attended the right schools, or because of their good looks, or amazing talent, will not have to endure such tests. Eddie Jemison, a well-known character actor living in LA says:

> *I was so stupid. I never did any real research . . . I struggled for years, doing cool things in college then sitting around doing nothing. I never did make it to New York. It took everything I had just to get by in Chicago. Of course, if I really knew what was in store for me, I would've either found a way to deny it, dismiss it or say, "It'll work out different for me." Delusion is a great tool for any young person looking for a start in the arts. Embrace it. If you don't, if you're too realistic you'll never do it.*

For some fortunate actors, work comes right away; they appear on major stages, get great TV series, or are cast as leads in films. It can happen that way. However, when the film has wrapped, when the series has folded, and the play has closed, these actors, like their brothers and sisters, are still left with the need to plan their survival. The stakes are high and, considering the difficult nature of our business in general, it seems only prudent to give yourself five years to achieve your dreams.

---

[4] IRS publication 535. An activity is presumed carried on for profit if it produced a profit in at least thee of the last five tax years, including the current year.

In May 2011 Bradley Cooper was interviewed by *Shave Magazine* online and asked how he felt about being considered a successful actor after *The Hangover* (2009) became a huge hit. He said:

> *It doesn't feel that way. Thank you for saying that. Not the case, I gotta say, but it certainly provided more opportunities. Everybody who was a part of that movie, because it was so financially lucrative, benefited from it but I still put myself on tape for movies and try to get roles. It's the same, you know? It's the same. I mean, look, more doors have been opened for sure but it's not like I sit back with a cigar on Monday morning and go through the scripts that have been offered—no, that's not the case.*

Your five-year plan: how to do it

It doesn't matter how you do this at first, but it is very important that you finally end up with a document that can be printed. Unlike handwritten lists and scraps of paper, when you print a document, there is something official and fulfilling about doing so.

1 Create a table using the six categories as headings. In the first column, **insert a date five years from NOW**. In this case, I will use 2020:

Future date	Artistic	Personal	Money	Day job	Education	Service
2020						

In order to fill in each category, you will need to prioritize your dreams. So, go back, review your dream lists, and number them in importance from one to six. You can keep your number ones and maybe a few twos. The rest may have to wait for a time—maybe put them on a potential ten-year list? Fill the table in to look like this:

	Artistic	Personal	Money	Day job	Education	Service
2020	Appear on Broadway. Start filming a movie with the Coen brothers.	Living in an apartment in Manhattan. Married, no kids, one dog.	Debt free. $30,000 in the bank.	Don't really need one, but I keep my skills up as a carpenter.	Taking classes at HB studios. Teaching myself to roast turkey.	Help disaster relief with my carpentry skills.

2 Describe clearly and frankly where you are NOW, in this case, 2015:

Now	Artistic	Personal	Money	Day Job	Education	Service
2015	Doing the showcase for school. Maybe going to get a job at a summer theatre. Living in Chicago.	Graduating in June. Living with a room-mate.	Income: $12,000. Student loans: $30,000. Yearly expenses: $18,000 (I get the rest from my parents).	Working at Subway.	Got my BFA. Want to take a Meisner class.	Participating in cleaning up the beach.

3 Merge the two rows and insert rows for each year between the NOW row and the FUTURE row:

	Artistic	Personal	Money	Day job	Education	Service
2020	Appear on Broadway. Start filming a movie with the Coen brothers.	Living in an apartment in Manhattan. Married, no kids, one dog.	Debt free. $30,000 in the bank.	Don't really need one, but I keep my skills up as a carpenter.	Taking classes at HB studios. Teaching myself to roast turkey.	Help disaster relief with my carpentry skills.
2019						
2018						
2017						
2016						
2015	Doing the showcase for school. Maybe going to get a job at a summer theatre. Living in Chicago.	Graduating in June. Living with a room-mate.	Income: $12,000. Student loans: $30,000. Yearly expenses: $18,000 (I get the rest from my parents).	Working at Subway.	Got my BFA. Want to take a Meisner class.	Participating in cleaning up the beach.

4 Look closely at the following pages. I have filled in the table to make it easier to understand. Staring at all of those years to fill in, it may feel impossible and overwhelming. Don't sweat it! You are simply creating scenarios, playing with what might happen, and how you might achieve some happiness in your Life Play. It's a big improv! Nothing is set in stone. Again, just give it the once-over. Don't get trapped in it. You aren't committing to anything. Just make it up. There is a delete button on all computers! Fill in the blanks as well as you can.

	Artistic	Personal	Money	Day Job	Educational	Service
2020	Appear on Broadway. Start filming a movie with the Coen brothers. Four commercials.	Living in an apartment in Manhattan. (Not gonna happen, how about Brooklyn?) Not married but thinking about it. No kids. One dog.	Debt free. $30,000 in the bank. (Not gonna happen this year unless I get really lucky) Total Income: $34,000. $20,000 B'dway. $4,000 film. $10,000 commercials.	Don't really need one, but I keep my skills up as a carpenter	Taking classes at HB studios. Teaching myself to roast turkey.	Help disaster relief with my carpentry skills.
2019	Appear in one-off Broadway show. Appear in a small but great role in a film. Do four national commercials.	Move to NYC with partner. Get an apartment. Keep the dog.	Pay $5,000 on loans. Use savings for move and apartment. Total Income: $20,000 Starbucks. $5,000 carpentry. $10,000 commercials.	Get work as a handyman or carpenter. Stay at Starbucks.	Take audition classes in NYC. Voice and movement classes.	Serve food to the homeless on Thanksgiving.
2018	Appear in three shows at major theatres, two musicals and one straight.	Stay in same apartment but with a significant other.	Pay $6,000 on my loans. Save $3,000. Total income $38,000.	Start working as a handyman/ carpenter.	Continue voice classes.	Continue working with kids in theatre.

(continued)

	Appear in a small but great role in a film. Three national commercials.	Keep the dog.	$20,000 Starbucks. $5,000 handyman. $6,000 from commercials. $1,000 from film. $6,000 for theatre.	Stay at Starbucks.	More dance classes.	
2017	Appear in two shows at major theatres. Appear in a small but great role in a series. Have two national commercials running.	Stay in same apartment but with a significant other. Keep the dog.	Pay $5,000 on my loans. Save $3,000. Total income: $32,000. $22,000 Starbucks. $4,000 from commercials. $1,000 from series. $5,000 from theatre.	Move up at Starbucks.	Continue voice classes. Take audition classes. Take jazz dance classes.	Work in the park or at church with kids for summer theatre workshops.
2016	Have an agent and be auditioning for major theatres. Also do two commercials. Be in two major theatre shows.	Stay with roommate. Get a dog.	Pay some on my loans. Save some. $20,000 from Starbucks. $2,000 from commercials.	Work at Starbucks.	In advanced Meisner class, also studying singing.	Working on the political campaign.
2015	Doing the showcase for school. Maybe going to get a job at a summer theatre. Living in Chicago.	Graduating in June. Living with a room-mate.	Income: $12,000. Student loans $30,000. Yearly expenses: 18,000 (I get the rest from my parents).	Working at Subway.	Got my BFA. Want to take a Meisner class.	Participating in cleaning up the beach.

More five-year plans

The plan following is one created by a graduate student who wants to move from acting to directing. His dream includes founding a theatre. As you can see he has some advanced skills for a day job, but he has been careful to anticipate paying off his student loan debt. He may be a bit too optimistic, but his plan seems doable! Maybe some of his dreams need to be put on a ten-year plan, and that is not a problem. He is aiming high and aiming for a specific goal. He has changed the plan categories to questions, and he has listed how old he will be in each year.

The plan is practical as well as ambitious. His hooking events to his age is a smart tactic. Benchmarking by age is a great idea! He clearly knows where he wants to be and what he wants to do.

	What are your artistic goals?	What are your personal goals?	What will you be doing for a job?	What are you education needs?	What is your debt/ financial situation?	What can you do for service work?
2016–17 How will you be? AGE: 32	Artistic director of a small physical theatre co.	Married. Paying a mortgage on a condo.	Salaried position w/ benefits w/ my theatre co.	Teaching workshop.	Three-quarters of school debt is paid off. Invested in IRA.	Volunteer at a local community garden.
2015–16 AGE: 31	Fundraising for opening of theatre. Gathering ensemble.	Putting in a bid on a condo.	Working a flex. full time Job at law firm w/ benefits.	Clowning workshop w/ Pig Iron Theatre.	Make double payments on school loans.	Volunteer at a local community garden.
2014–15 MOVE TO WASH DC AGE: 30	Perform at Woolly Mammoth in DC.	Move with partner to DC.	Get in with good temp agency to secure job. Receive NEA grant.	On-camera class.	Half of school debt paid.	Food shelter.
2013–14 AGE: 29	Theatres: Lookingglass Hypocrites New Colony Dog and Pony Book a Commercial	Live with roomie. Have a partner.	Flex full time with benefits.	SITI summer intensive.	Pay all credit cards and make more than minimum on loans.	SPCA.
The present year: 2012–13 AGE: 28	All general auditions done and signed with agent by March.	Living with roomie	Get in with temp agency.	Training year at the Actors' Gym.	$35,000 school loans, $1,000 credit card.	Community garden.

As you make your plan, consider where you passions are and make them as specific as possible. If you discover after crafting this document that your dreams seem to be clearer for you in areas outside of performing, perhaps that is a sign for you. Be honest with yourself—if you can't see yourself in the profession, it may be that you would be happier doing something else. If you lie to yourself and half-heartedly pursue an acting career, you may end up bitter and broke five years hence. Don't plan to fail, as the young woman on the next several page, Mary, seems to have done.

Year	Artistic	Personal	Debt/finance	Day job	Education	Service
5	Use the talents that I have around me to begin to create some sort of documentary. Be in a feature film.	Married to whomever and settled in a beautiful home in Maryland. Be members of a church home that we both agree upon. Take a summer off to travel different places all over the world and soak up different cultures and really expand on my writing.	I plan to be $9,200 dollars in debt. I plan to pay this $9,200 off before the year is up.	Be a full-time actress.	Fluent in Spanish. Proficient in over fifteen dialects. 500 poems in five years. Write a book, a play, or a screenplay.	Have a solid ground plan and mission statement down for my organization, begin to promote the idea and see who I can get on board. Run in the breast cancer awareness marathon.
4	Make more friends in the business, and have a professional reel sent out.	Have my own car, and a really nice apartment/ condo where I live alone. Continuing to build my relationship with God and being a consistent tither. Make sure both my parents are on their feet and stable.	I plan to be $18,400 in debt.	Finish out the year at Robinson Center and give my letter of resignation.	Begin to learn Spanish and ballroom dancing.	Organize my team of people on board to help with my community organization and begin to search for grants.

Year	Artistic	Personal	Debt/finance	Day job	Education	Service
3	Become SAG, and begin to audition for film and large equity theatres in New York and Chicago.	Build my relationship with my father's side of the family.	I plan to be $27,600 in debt.	Take more offsite projects at Robinson Center, giving myself more freedom to do shows.	Document and film my grandmother's story before anything happens to her.	Develop my dream for my own community organization, for example where I want to be located and my target community and goal.
2	Book a commercial gig. Begin to do some indie film in order to get a feel for the camera and make a reel.	Work on starting and maintaining a relationship with someone I care about. Putting aside time for a significant other.	I plan to be $36,800 in debt.	Because of shows I will hopefully be able to quit my waitress position and use that night-time hour to learn lines and also get my name out there.	Work on building and maintaining a blog. Journal about EVERYTHING in hopes to form a play or book in 2016.	Form groups of four or more people to go to the community organizations that I am already in contact with. Show them my dedication and continued support while continuing to learn more about building and maintaining a community organization.

(continued)

Year	Artistic	Personal	Debt/finance	Day job	Education	Service
1	Start auditioning and working for theatres like Goodman Court and Steppenwolf. Be Equity by the end of 2012.	Create a life after college for myself here in Chicago. Help my mother get her GED. Apply for Teach for America and Baltimore Teaching Residency as back up plans. Have my hair be 100 percent natural and be at a solid size 5.	I am $46,000 in debt, which I plan to pay off in five years. Therefore I must pay: $766.66 per month to reach that goal. It is possible. By the end of the six-month grace period I will have six months of payments on my student loans. Until I can find another way I will have to pay over $700 dollars a month to Sallie Mae. I plan to save money on rent by living with my	Become full-time at the Robinson Center and have a flexible schedule where I can audition when necessary. Also find night-time work as a waitress/hostess and/or babysitting.	Be the first woman in my family to graduate college. Continue to diversify and categorize my play database. Began to incorporate screenplays. Study and create an easy access database to directors, producers, and actors I want to work with. Apply for Yale's graduate school as an option. If I do that I will have to create a	Become a regular volunteer at Arts of life, LVEJO, Voices for Creative Non-Violence. Work with the Greater Chicago Food Depository, T. Along with my service I will ask questions and take notes on building a community organization, maintaining one, and how I can start mine in years to come.

Year	Artistic	Personal	Debt/finance	Day job	Education	Service
			brother, paying him extra cash whenever I get money. Whatever money I get for my graduation, I will put that towards paying off my loans.		new five-year plan!!	

In looking at her plan what jumps out at me is her dedication to family life and to her writing/academic life. Her clearest vision seems to be in the areas of self-enrichment and documentary-making. Details regarding her acting life are unclear, lacking passion. She seems to have an idea of how to begin but no discernible follow-through in that area. It is clear that she doesn't understand that once she has auditioned for larger theatres and perhaps been cast in them, she needs to build on those achievements in the following years.

In the first year of her artistic plan, she is very definite concerning the theatres in which she wishes to work, but she has not included the building blocks needed to be hired by those top-tier Equity houses nor how she might obtain an AEA card. She has not even mentioned getting an agent. The second year doesn't mention theatre at all, only one commercial and a lackluster comment about beginning to do some "indie film." Likewise in her third year, she says she wants to become SAG, but there is no plan for it unless she decides to do more commercials or to move up in the film world. Her fourth year is definitely underfunded, finding friends should have happened along the way, and without a significant body of film work she will be unable to develop a reel. Her fifth year is so non-specific that I doubt that she will ever get to that place because her vision for her artistic life is so limited.

Perhaps Mary is frightened—notice that in the first year out of her training program, she wants to run back into school. She says she wants to apply to Yale as well as applying to Teach for America and for a Baltimore Teaching Residency. All three of these things would preclude any other career involvement. And all of them would keep her safely in the classroom for a longer time. She seems to lack any faith that she might be able to make a living in her chosen career.

Applying to Yale and other places is premature, but it may be that she is more interested in stability than in having a genuine acting career. With this little forethought, Mary is going to have a very hard time. For instance, while she says that she wants to be married, live in Maryland and travel in her fifth year, none of it is accounted for in this plan in terms of debt or jobs. And, while it is very possible to be a full-time actress in the Baltimore/DC area, it is going to take a lot of preparation in that market to do so. In the third year she also says that she wants to audition for theatres in New York, but again there is no plan for a move. She is definitely scattered.

Is it possible that Mary is like many acting students in that she loved being in plays at school, but never believed that she would do anything but amateur theatre once she graduated. Are you one of those people? If you are, don't be ashamed of it! Plan to have the life that you want, not the life that you said you wanted when you first started taking classes. No one will blame you for it and you won't have to waste your time and money on something for which you no longer have a passion.

When I was doing theatre, I did feel like I was giving up part of my life to be an actor. I went from show to show to show for five straight years out of college. I had a boyfriend at the time (now my husband) who had a nine to five job, and I missed being home with him on nights, weekends and holidays. Even before I met him, my passion for theatre was diminishing, so it was easy for me to say I want to take a break and spend more time with him. Seven years later, I am happy doing a project here or there and focusing on voiceover, on-camera, and my other dream job as a life coach. I was afraid others would think I gave up but I know I just changed my mind. I've definitely enjoyed the schedule more, and the increase in income, but I think I am getting an itch to return to the stage right now.

COURTNEY RIOUX HUBBARD, life coach, voiceover

One of the best five-year plans I have seen is the one that follows. This actor made his own format, and it suited him. I have no problem in changing forms when someone is so able to organize his or her ideas. I do wish he had planned some community service, but that is not what he wanted to focus on. This actor is so passionate that he is able to understand what he wants and so he has made the format fit him. Pay attention to the amount of detail in all the areas he has chosen. Because of his ability to plan, and his careful strategy, I am pleased to say that he has accomplished almost all of the things he wanted to do at the time of writing and is well ahead of himself in many areas.

Target theatre companies: Goodman, Steppenwolf, Remy Bumppo, Lookingglass, TimeLine, Northlight, Chicago Shakes, Porchlight, Writer's Theatre, Hypocrites.

	Artistic	Money	Personal
2016	Free to choose in Chicago. Member of SAG and AEA. Free to change cities if I want.	Complete financial independence from parents. Student loans completely paid off. Health insurance.	Free to choose housing and bar employment. Musical proficiency. Language proficiency in Spanish and French.
2015–16	1+ show in New York.	Commercial/TV/ Film (50%/$25,000).	Move into great apartment.
	2+ plays for target companies and/ or regional.	Theatre (10%/$5,000).	Guitar practice.
	5+ jobs in commercial, film, TV and VO.	Social networking for 3 clients (20%/$10,000).	Piano practice.
		Bartending (20%/$10,000).	Spanish proficiency.
		INCOME = $50,000.	French proficiency.
		Rent and Utilities: –$9,600 ($800/mo).	Regular cardio and weights.
		Student loans: –$3,600 ($300/mo).	
		Retirement acct: –$2,000.	
		LIVING = $34,800.	

Target theatre companies: Goodman, Steppenwolf, Remy Bumppo, Lookingglass, TimeLine, Northlight, Chicago Shakes, Porchlight, Writer's Theatre, Hypocrites

	Artistic	Money	Personal
2014 –15	1+ play for target theatre companies.	Commercial/TV/film (30%/$13,500).	Find a new bar.
	2+ plays for regional theatre companies.	Theatre (10%/$4,500).	Guitar practice.
	5+ jobs in commercial, film, TV and VO.	Social networking for 4 clients (25%/$11,250).	Piano practice.
	1+ musical.	Bartending (40%/$18,000).	Spanish proficiency.
	Join Actors Equity.	INCOME = $45,000.	French proficiency.
		Rent and utilities: –$9,600 ($800/mo).	Regular cardio and weights.
		Student loans: –$3,600 ($300/mo).	
		Retirement Acct: –$2,000.	
		LIVING = $29,800.	
2013 –14	2+ plays at target theatre companies.	Commercial/TV/film (20%/$8,000).	New place summer of 2013.
	1+ play at a regional theatre company.	Social networking for 5 clients (30%/$12,000).	Guitar practice.
	5+ jobs in commercial, film, TV or VO.	Bartending (50%/$20,000).	Piano practice.

(continued)

Target theatre companies: Goodman, Steppenwolf, Remy Bumppo, Lookingglass, TimeLine, Northlight, Chicago Shakes, Porchlight, Writer's Theatre, Hypocrites

	Artistic	Money	Personal
		INCOME = $40,000.	Spanish proficiency.
		Rent and utilities: –$9,600 ($800/mo).	French proficiency.
		Student loans: –$3,600 ($300/mo).	Regular cardio and weights.
		Retirement Acct: –$1,500.	
		LIVING = $25,300.	
2012–13	Do a play with Goodman, Shakes or Steppenwolf.	Commercial/TV/film (10%/$3,500).	Guitar proficiency.
	2+ plays at target theatre companies.	Social networking for 3 clients (25%/$9,600).	Piano practice.
	3+ jobs in commercial, film, TV or VO.	Steady bartender by summer 2013 (65%/$21,900).	Regular cardio and weights.
	1+ musical.	INCOME = $35,000.	Spanish proficiency.
	Join SAG.	Rent and utilities: –$7,800 ($650/mo).	Basic French speaking ability.
		Student loans: –$3,000 ($250/mo).	
		Retirement Acct: –$1,500.	
		LIVING = $22,700.	

Target theatre companies: Goodman, Steppenwolf, Remy Bumppo, Lookingglass, TimeLine, Northlight, Chicago Shakes, Porchlight, Writer's Theatre, Hypocrites

	Artistic	Money	Personal
2011 –12	Agent by September.	Commercial/TV/film (5%/$1,200).	Guitar lessons.
	2–5 plays at small theatre co.	Social networking for 2 clients (20%/$4,800).	Piano repertoire (12–15 songs).
	Do a play with TimeLine Theatre.	Steady bar back by summer 2012 (75%/$18,000).	Regular cardio and weights.
	Understudy for Goodman, Shakes or Steppenwolf.	INCOME = $24,000.	Basic Spanish speaking ability.
	At least 1 job in commercial, film, TV or VO.	Rent and utilities: –$7,800 ($650/mo).	
	Complete a film reel.	Student Loans: –$2,400 ($200/mo).	
	Build a website.	Retirement Acct: –$1,000	
	Postcards	LIVING = $12,800	

My five-year plan

Many of you look at the charts. Looking at the charts can be overwhelming. The task may seem so difficult. However, remember when your "civilian" friends ask you, "How do you remember all those lines?" Most acters laugh. Few can actually answer this question, but most actors know that it is simply a matter of beginning and working moment-by-moment, beat-by-beat, scene-by-scene, act-by-act and somehow it all falls into place. Think of this assignment in the same way. You don't have to get it right all at once. You will make mistakes and have to go back and look again. You will forget things that you need to remember, but sooner or later, you will complete your script. Because that is what a five-year plan is—the script of your Life Play.

4

Making Your Five-Act Life Play Happen

Remember, you can't do a five-act play in one fell swoop. It must be tackled act-by-act, scene-by-scene. Please don't be too frightened of planning. Some of you will love making these appointments with yourself but others will be overwhelmed by the task and decide to simply take their chances. President John F. Kennedy said it well: "Effort and courage are not enough without purpose and direction." For those of you who are among the overwhelmed, you might consider that if you don't make some small attempt to plan on a monthly or seasonal basis, life will plan for you. Now *is* the time of your life. You have spent a lot of it training, and now is not the time to sit back and let the world come to you. It won't. As Lady Macbeth says to Macbeth, ". . . screw your courage to the sticking post and you'll not fail."

If you have been keeping your life in your head, that is a waste of space and only adds static and the possibility of forgetting. Put it on paper! Whether you like to keep a handwritten calendar, or a calendar on your computer, you should enter all of your tasks on it. I use the calendar that comes with my Gmail account, and color code different responsibilities on the days I need to do them—i.e. yellow for directing, green for classes, red for writing, and so on.

Begin by looking at what you want to have accomplished in the year *after* you finish your training. Let's begin with your artistic dreams. In my examples, I will use a June-to-June schedule because so many of us see the world in that way, but do what seems right for you. Ideally you should begin with the month and market in which you are committed to starting a career in earnest. So, if you decide to take a nice long holiday following your training, don't begin until after you return. Leaving a market when you have just begun is the surest road to disaster. Once you are represented by an agent, be aware that you will need to be available for most of the next two years. As you prepare your plan, you will always be working backwards in a way. Getting to the fifth year means building from the first year to the second, and so on.

Below is a copy of the first two years of artistic dreams from our yearly calendar example. Notice that this actor (you) wants to do two commercials in 2016 in Chicago. You will therefore need an agent because that is how commercials are cast. (If you have one, it may also assist you in getting theatre jobs in that market, but every city will differ in that area.) So, you will need representation by that time, and you should probably form a relationship with an agency before January 2016.

Artistic

2016   Have an agent and be auditioning for major theatres.
         Also do two commercials.
         Be in two major theatre shows.

Now   Doing the showcase for school.
         Maybe trying to get a job at a summer theatre.

Theatre, TV, and commercials are rather seasonal. Commercial production companies and advertising agencies tend to follow the school year with summers being a bit dead. Also, as in theatre, the weeks between Thanksgiving and the New Year feature few auditions. In the commercial world, there can be a last-minute rush in mid-December to spend any remaining budgets that the advertising agencies have been allotted, but that is not as predictable as the summer slump.

Television series have a similar "school year" sort of schedule with the exception of "pilot season," which has traditionally been late January through mid-April. While I suspect that you know this already, a "pilot" is simply one episode of a show that is used to test whether a program has enough interest for the producers to gamble on further production. Because of the obvious changes in TV viewing habits, the proliferation of means to view a show, and the availability of viewer data, programmers are increasingly abandoning pilots and going directly into production. The number of pilots commissioned by a network or independent channels are therefore fewer than in the past. Be that as it may, for the time being many pilots will still be cast in the early part of the year. Pilots are cast throughout the country, so if you don't go to LA, your local casting office may be covering them, or your agent may be taping and submitting you for shows as well. If series work is your aim, it would be best therefore if you had an agent before pilot season. When agents are too busy to see you, it is not a great time to try to get one. Of course, it can be done, but it may take a bit longer.

What will you need to do to ensure that your dreams come true? As in a scene, you will need to do one *logical action* after another in response to what the people in your world are presenting to you. You finish one scene before you move to the next.

Logical actions to get an agent, more or less in order

1 Get a good picture and résumé to present to agents.

2 Research what agencies might be interested in you and what their specialities are if they have one (this will be discussed in the chapter on agents and casting directors).

3 Make contact with various agencies.

4 Meet with agents.

5 After that, it is more or less out of your hands. An agent may be interested in representing you or not. But you have done your work, and even if you are not asked to sign, he or she may ask that you stay in touch. Do so! It is not unusual for agents to work on a freelance basis with an actor until such time as they are sure that the fit is good.

For your scheduling plan, make a *guestimate* of how long it might take you to accomplish these things and write down the days you think you might be able to do the following activities.

June 15–July 15: research agents, both online and through other actors. Looking at an agent's list of talent (that is what they call actors) can help you to see if they have a lot of people "just like you" or only a few. It can also assist you in determining how the agency wishes to be perceived, and what kinds of people they represent. Talking to other actors is also a good way to discover if an agent may be right for you.

June 15–June 30: research online, and call agencies to enquire what photographers they prefer. Realize that you will probably not be able to speak directly to an agent, but don't be discouraged. Be very nice, the person who answers the phone may own the agency next year. These folks may help or not, but try anyway. Make sure you get their names and put them in your contact list with a note concerning your conversation including the date. You will be calling them again!

Logical actions to make the agency thing happen after doing your research

June 30	Make appointments to meet several photographers if you can stand the pressure.
July 1–5	Meet with photographers to determine with whom you feel most comfortable. You should ask what markets they think you might work in. Also consult about wardrobe and hair at this time because it will help you to see how the photographer envisions you.
July 6	Make an appointment with your chosen picture-taker. Have a haircut/style if needed.
July 8	Gather wardrobe for pictures. If possible take pictures of yourself in various garments to see how they work.
July 10	If possible, do a mock photo session with a friend.
July 15	Have pictures done.
July 18	Draw up a résumé.
July 20	When you get your proofs, consult with people you know in the business concerning your best headshots by either sending them the thumbnails or directing them to the website the photographer uses for the purpose. If you don't know anyone yet, check to see if your mother loves the picture. If she does, it is probably not the one you want to use (more in the chapter on headshots and résumés).

July 25–Aug 25	Meet agents where possible, bringing a few of your headshot choices and a résumé as well as a disk of your proofs (see casting director and agency chapters).
	Send thank-you notes to agents you have met and add them along with details of your conversation and observations to your contact list.
Aug 25	Sign with agent or make an agreement to freelance if possible.
Aug 30	Have as many pictures printed as your agent requests, making sure that you have enough to take to auditions.

Does this make you crazy? If you really think about it, most of these things don't take a lot of time. Remember, in order to use the training in which you have invested so much time, effort, and money, it is the least you can do for yourself.

Another example: in the five-year plan example, the actor in question states that he wants to be in two plays in 2016 in major theatres. What should be done? Most actors will hope to be called in, maybe send a picture and—and pray. According to what I have heard, "God helps those that help themselves." If you want to do a play at a particular theatre in their fall season which opens September 20, 2016 and runs through November 20, 2016, you will need to make a plan of attack quite a bit earlier than you might suspect. Luckily you already have your pictures and your résumé as well as an agent. So, depending on the size of the theatre, and how far in advance they choose their season, you might need to prepare in January of 2016 to be sure of being considered for a role in the fall.

Logical actions to take to get a job at a desired theatre, no particular order

1   Send picture and résumé with a query letter in the spring.

2   Read all of the plays in the season if possible.

3   Investigate whether the play is precast.

4 Find out if the theatre holds auditions by appointment or as a part of a general call.

5 Research the director and the company doing the show.

As you can see, it might be smarter to reorder this 'top of the head' list before proceeding to spare yourself unnecessary work. This kind of planning can help you to find mistakes and give you more ideas about approaching the job.

Logical actions to take to get a job at a desired theatre in a sensible order

1 Read all of the plays in the season if possible, to see if there is a role for you.

2 Research the director and the company doing the show. Look at their website and read their statement of purpose or philosophy.

3 Investigate whether the play is precast with company members, or relatives of the director.

4 Find out if the theatre is going to be holding auditions by appointment, or as a part of a general call.

5 Send a P&R with a pointed query letter in the summer.

6 If you have an agent, make sure that he or she suggests you to the person responsible for casting.

Why should you read the plays first and investigate the company and the director? Because not only will you want to see if there is something that you could conceivably play, but in order to write a letter to the director or casting director, you need to be familiar enough to tell them specifically why you would be helpful in the project, and what role you would like to be read for. If on reading the plays in their season you find that you aren't castable in them because of age or for whatever reason, you can move on to other things.

Now add the dates when you intend to do these tasks to your calendar. You must painstakingly make appointments to meet the future. If you were still in school, you would have to do this in the same way for assignments. Now that you are no longer a student, preparation is even more important.

January 21–25 (or when season is announced)	21 Visit all webpages of the theatres you are interested in to discover what their season will be. If possible, investigate how much of the season is precast.
	22 Research the director and the company doing the show. Is the company a consortium of actors whose ages are similar to yours?
	23 If you have never auditioned for the company or director, try to see if and when they hold general auditions.
	25 Get the plays that are not precast, or in the case of a new play, investigate the author.
February 5–15	Read the plays to see if there is a role for you. If you can't obtain the script and if it has been produced in the past, Google past performances and reviews.
March 25	Send a P&R with a pointed query letter to the casting director in the late summer.
	Tell your agent that you have sent a query letter and make sure that he or she is aware of your interest.
March 28	Write a personal note to the director telling them why you are interested in the show and in working with them specifically.

5

Handling the Obstacles in Your Life Play

Theoretically, you have created your plan in macro, done beautiful lists, and now it is time to do the *micro*. As Stanislavski says, "The general is the death of art." He means that without fully examining a play or a role in depth, nothing can be accomplished. The same is true for your Life Play. This chapter will present a more detailed approach to elements that might trip you up in your everyday life.

While we have been working on this book, my associate, Jacob Stanton, and I have been discussing the problem that presents the biggest obstacle for actors. That is the problem of *accessibility*: access to agents, casting directors, directors, and the information about who is who, who is doing what, and where they are doing it. The adage "It's who you know" is absolutely and vitally true. The ability to enter the business and to stay in it depends on creating relationships with the people who represent actors, who direct actors, and who hire them. Additionally you need to know the rules of the game that vary from region to region and from medium to medium.

To a great extent, accessibility is limited by money, education, and time. If you really think about it, both education and time depend on having sufficient money. For that reason, the first order of business is to look at your finances—they will probably be your biggest obstacle; how much money you have, how to get more, and how much things cost.

Student loans

For many of you, student loans are the largest debt you have. (I will deal with credit card debt later in this section.) Therefore, it is necessary to determine exactly how much you will owe for your education. Many students, both in the arts and otherwise, are frightened to look at the figures; they prefer not to know, even when they themselves are responsible for the loans. For some lucky students, their parents have been taking care of all of it. Whatever your situation, now that you are grown up, you need to know whether the debt is on your shoulders alone, or on your parents, or kindly uncles and aunts, or grandparents. About ten years ago, I had a very talented student, a single mom, who was trying to get through the university as a theatre major. Recently she wrote:

> I owe Fannie Mae about $50,000, which was as much as I could borrow, but it didn't allow me to finish school, and I haven't paid into it [bitter and angry and poor]. My intention has always been to begin paying it back when I don't have to live paycheck to paycheck. I did have a lot of family support, well, at least support from my mother. Student loans helped pay for school, and rent, but as I was also a single mother, a great deal of my son's clothes, shoes, tuition and so forth, came from my mother. And even with that support, I got into this debt.

This young woman is just like many of you, she didn't want to look at the consequences of her actions. She relied on fate, which is seldom kind. Go to the financial aid office at your school and ask. There are many different types of federal student loans and they all have different rules and regulations. The financial aid office should be able to tell you the kind of loan or loans, federal or private, that you have and the interest entailed. They will also let you know whether the type of loan you have has a grace period. Some loans have an interest-free grace period, some don't, some grace periods are longer, some shorter. Be sure you understand your own situation NOW, so that you can plan more effectively.

The interest rate on any loan is set when you first take out that particular loan, and if you take out more loans the interest rates are determined for them at that time. Unlike private loans, you don't have the option of declaring bankruptcy on federal student loans. It is important that you know which loans are federal and which are private. They all have different ways of calculating interest. Once you have discovered the exact amount you owe, along with the interest rates attached to each of your loans and their peculiarities, you can then decide how and when you will be able to free yourself of this burden.

First let's look at federal loans. I have gotten almost all of this information on the government's student loan website and I urge you to visit it: **https://studentaid.ed.gov**. It is an easy to read site, very user friendly, and covers an enormous amount of financial territory.

The interest rate on federal student loans depends on the type of federal loan you have, but currently the rates vary from 3.85 percent to 7.21 percent and are computed daily based on the amount you owe, plus interest. It is easy to forget about *amortization*. Don't stop reading here, I know it's intimidating, but if I can figure this out, so can you! Amortization is the practice of spreading out payments over a given amount of time, say twelve months. This is helpful for you because you don't have to come up with great big payments at the end of the year. However, it will cost you.

Here is an example of how *simple interest* accrues. I am using only increments of "10s" because they are easier to see. If you have taken a loan amounting to $10,000, using simple interest at 10 percent, to discharge the debt in one year with one payment at the end of the year you would pay $10,000 (the principal) plus $1,000 in interest added in that first year, for a total of $11,000. Simple? Not so simple. This example disregards the reality of banking practices.

For most of you, it is more likely that you would pay your loan off monthly with twelve payments of about $879.16/month (based upon simple interest loan *plus amortization*) for a total payment amount of $10,549.92, meaning that it's cheaper to pay monthly than yearly.

For most of you, such high payments at the beginning of a career are very difficult to make. So, if you take five years to pay, or sixty monthly payments of about $212.47/month, you would end up paying $12,748.20 owing to the interest that accrues over sixty months. This may be worth it because you are essentially buying the comfort of lower monthly obligations.

Some of you may be able to have your loan payments postponed for an amount of time depending on the type of loan you have been given. This is called a *deferment*. There is also a program using the term *forbearance* which is generally for a twelve-month period and differs from a deferment owing to the type of loan, the individual's work situation, health and so on. In both types of postponements, interest rates may accrue to be added to the amount of the loan. The rules that govern this assistance are at **https://studentaid.ed.gov/**.

WARNING! If you make no payments on your $10,000, 10 percent, five-year loan until the end of year five, you would end up paying about $16,453.09 assuming monthly capitalization of interest. The differences are significant. Look at the examples below:

Twelve months with monthly payments would cost:	$549.00
Twelve months with no payment till the end would cost:	$1,000.00
Sixty months with monthly payments would cost:	$2,748.00
Sixty months with no payment till the end would cost:	$6,453.09

If you don't pay on time, or if you underpay, penalties will accrue. These fees will be added to the principal amount of the loan depending on the policies of the loan. The adage that "time is money" applies to this particular human interaction.

These facts should lead you to realize that you need either to find a way to lower your interest rates, or to pay off your loans quickly. The following chart published by the Federal Student Loan Program on its website gives you the variety of ways that you might pay off a federal loan depending on the type of loan. The site also includes a discussion of the differences between each repayment program and their requirements.

Given the realities of student loan amounts and the interest rates, it is to your advantage to find a way to deal with them *sooner* rather than later. Do not decide that this is all too complicated and that someday in the future when you are a wealthy star, someone will figure out how to make all of this go away!

The free Federal Consolidation Loan Program can be beneficial depending on your situation. *Consolidating* means that you get to take out one great big loan to pay off all your federal student debt,

Paying off a federal loan

Repayment plan	Eligible loans	Monthly payment and time frame	Quick comparison
Standard Repayment Plan	Direct subsidized and unsubsidized loans Subsidized and unsubsidized Federal Stafford loans all PLUS loans	Payments are a fixed amount of at least $50 per month Up to 10 years	You'll pay less interest for your loan over time under this plan than you would under other plans.
Graduated Repayment Plan	Direct subsidized and unsubsidized loans Subsidized and unsubsidized Federal Stafford Loans all PLUS loans	Payments are lower at first and then increase, usually every two years Up to ten years	You'll pay more for your loan over time than under the 10-year standard plan.
Extended Repayment Plan	Direct subsidized and unsubsidized loans Subsidized and unsubsidized Federal Stafford loans all PLUS loans	Payments may be fixed or graduated Up to 25 years	Your monthly payments would be lower than the 10-year standard plan. If you are a direct loan borrower, you must have more than $30,000 in outstanding direct Loans. FFEL borrower, you must have more than $30,000 in outstanding FFEL Program loans. For example, if you have $35,000 in outstanding FFEL Program loans, and $10,000 in direct loans, you can use the extended repayment plan for your FFEL Program loans, but not for your direct loans.

			For both programs, you must also be a "new borrower" as of October 7, 1998. You'll pay more for your loan over time than under the 10-year standard plan.
Income-Based Repayment Plan (IBR)	Direct subsidized and unsubsidized loans Subsidized and unsubsidized Federal Stafford loans all PLUS loans made to students Consolidation loans (direct or FFEL) that do not include direct or FFEL PLUS loans made to parents	Your maximum monthly payments will be 15 percent of discretionary income, the difference between your adjusted gross income and 150 percent of the poverty guideline for your family size and state of residence (other conditions apply) Your payments change as your income changes Up to 25 years	You must have a partial financial hardship. Your monthly payments will be lower than payments under the 10-year standard plan. You'll pay more for your loan over time than you would under the 10-year standard plan. If you have not repaid your loan in full after making the equivalent of 25 years of qualifying monthly payments, any outstanding balance on your loan will be forgiven. You may have to pay income tax on any amount that is forgiven.
Pay As You Earn Repayment Plan	Direct subsidized and unsubsidized loans Direct PLUS loans made to students Direct consolidation loans that do not include (Direct or	Your maximum monthly payments will be 10 percent of discretionary income, the difference between your adjusted gross income and 150 percent of the poverty guideline for your family size and	You must be a new borrower on or after October 1, 2007, and must have received a disbursement of a direct loan on or after October 1, 2011. You must have a partial financial hardship. Your monthly payments will be lower than payments under the 10-year standard plan.

(continued)

Repayment plan	Eligible loans	Monthly payment and time frame	Quick comparison
	FFEL) PLUS loans made to parents	state of residence (other conditions apply). Your payments change as your income changes. Up to 20 years	You'll pay more for your loan over time than you would under the 10-year standard plan. If you have not repaid your loan in full after you made the equivalent of 20 years of qualifying monthly payments, any outstanding balance on your loan will be forgiven. You may have to pay income tax on any amount that is forgiven.
Income-Contingent Repayment Plan	Direct subsidized and unsubsidized loans Direct PLUS loans made to students Direct consolidation Loans	Payments are calculated each year and are based on your adjusted gross income, family size, and the total amount of your direct loans. Your payments change as your income changes. Up to 25 years	You'll pay more for your loan over time than under the 10-year standard plan. If you do not repay your loan after making the equivalent of 25 years of qualifying monthly payments, the unpaid portion will be forgiven. You may have to pay income tax on the amount that is forgiven.

| Income-Sensitive Repayment Plan | Subsidized and unsubsidized Federal Stafford loans FFEL PLUS loans FFEL consolidation loans | Your monthly payment is based on annual income. Your payments change as your income changes. Up to 10 years | You'll pay more for your loan over time than you would under the 10-year standard plan. Each lender's formula for determining the monthly payment amount under this plan can vary. |

Most readers of this book probably took out loans somewhere between 2009 and 2012.
The figures below give the interest rates as of 2013 for loans taken out after 2008.

Direct Subsidized undergraduate loans

First disbursement between 7/1/08-6/30/09: 6.00%
First disbursement between 7/1/09-6/30/10: 5.60%
First disbursement between 7/1/10-6/30/11: 4.50%
First disbursement between 7/1/11-6/30/12: 3.40%

Unsubsidized loans, graduate loans, and all other subsidized loans not included above: 6.80%

hopefully at a lower interest rate. You will still owe the amount you have incurred for the principal, as well as the interest you owed at the time you consolidated, but such a loan *may* give you a lower rate overall, and therefore allow you to breathe a bit more freely.

The rate for a federal consolidated loan is based on what is called a "weighted average" interest rate for the loans that you are bundling. When you apply for a consolidation loan, the new interest rate will be assigned depending on the amount of the loans and the interest rates for each separate loan. There are requirements for consolidating that you can find listed on the federal student loan website.

Another way to lower your interest rate is to make a deal with a friend or a family member who has savings and investments (if you are lucky enough to have these kinds of relatives), and who might lend you the full amount, allowing you to repay the debt at a lower interest rate. I suggest that if you do have such a relative, you approach them not with your hand out, but as a person who wants to make a business offer. Such an approach may not seem very "family friendly" but it might just help you to pay off your loan, and also allow your family to see your ability to deal with the world as an adult. It may even be that the person whom you approach will give you better terms than your offer. The most important thing is to have a written contract between the two of you to avoid the disaster of entitlements and misunderstandings that could cause no end of trouble for you and yours.

Regardless of how you choose to repay your federal loans, there are some advantages to keeping them, and paying off any private loans more quickly. Many private loans don't have a fixed interest rate, and the interest that you pay is *not deductible from your taxes*. The interest on federal student loans can be deducted, which can help offset the very cost of the interest itself.

Private student loans

These types of loans are those taken out by you or your parents from a private bank or other lending institution. In general, they have higher interest rates than federal loans. Such lending institutions may charge fixed interest rates, simple interest rates, or variable interest rates.

Such rates can go up or down depending on the economy. This fluctuation can be hazardous to your economic health. Some variable rate loans only change once a year, but others may have less predictable time restrictions. Private loans also carry fees and late payment penalties. These loans, whether variable or not, are granted based on the credit rating of the borrower. If you and yours don't have great credit, you will pay more. As with your federal loans, you must discover exactly what you owe to what institution and how much you are being charged for the right to have used their money. Your life will be increasingly dependent on a good credit rating and paying off loans is a good way to achieve one.

Credit card debt

We live in the digital age, and most of us depend on our credit cards. We don't carry a lot of cash around, and we may even receive our wages and pay our bills using direct deposit and instant payments through our banks. This is all very convenient but can also be crippling because it is so tempting not to look at the statements you are receiving either by mail or online, and to pay only the minimum necessary. After your credit card arrives in the mail, are you too frightened to actually look at the percentage rates and all those odd notices sent by the company? The rules of interest say that continuing to ignore such things will drive you to the brink of disaster. When the time comes to give back the gold at the end of the rainbow and you are not able to do so, you will receive endless voicemails from unknown callers leaving you very unpleasant dunning messages.

When you don't respond, these lovely people will begin to contact your family and your employers and demand that their money plus penalties be deducted from your wages. Just like anything in life, inattention and neglect will inevitably end in deterioration and failure. You are the person who spent the money. They lent it to you and charged a rate to do so. You signed some sort of an agreement in a moment of recklessness indicating that you would pay the money back with interest. The time will come when the piper must be paid. The only solution is facing your debt squarely and making a plan to eliminate it.

Again, from another student who kindly shared his story:

I completely destroyed my credit when I was nineteen and defaulted on some credit cards, because "I had no other options" which really meant I didn't know my options. To this day over a decade later I still cannot qualify by myself for any type of loan, be it car, house, small business or for continued education. This has severely limited my options post under-graduation, and even having been accepted to grad schools there is no way for me to pay for it out of pocket.

I did not understand how credit worked and how it affected your life. It is absolutely false that bad credit disappears after seven years in your report, the companies all have loopholes that prevent that from actually occurring. It stays with you forever. Even if you pay it off and settle or get credit counseling, the report still shows you settled for less than the old amount and it affects your credit. Avoid debt at all costs and if you have to take it DO NOT DEFAULT!

I don't share this as some sort of sob story or pity play. I learned some lessons the real hard way and I hope that this lesson can help some of your students avoid the same fate.

I suggest that you destroy all but *one* credit card (the one with the lowest interest rate), and pay off the ones you have stopped using as soon as you can. Pay the full balance on the one you keep each month. In an ideal world, once the old cards are paid off, you should pay the balance on your *only* card every month. Use cash or checks for most things, and set up automatic deductions from your bank account for your rent, your car payments, and other essential monthly expenses. If you monitor your bank account online, you can actually watch your financial life passing before your eyes.

If you find that you cannot pay off your card monthly once the others are handled, you will have to cut your expenses or negotiate a better deal with your *one* card's lender. You can do this; it has been known to happen. Figure it this way. When a lender gives you money, they are taking a chance on your success in life. They want and need you to prosper. If you have been making every effort to pay off your card and simply can't do it, it is best to call them and ask for a lower rate. Tell them that you have eliminated all but their card and want to make a fair deal. If this doesn't work, shop for a new card with a lower rate. These rates are published online every day. Try **nerdwallet.com**. Credit card companies are competitive and offer new rates all the time. Be sure you read the fine print, there can be lots of hidden fees. Do not live a life where you are still paying interest on the beer and hamburger you ate six months ago.

If you can join a credit union, do so, most of them offer very low interest cards and you may even be able to transfer your debt at a better rate than the *one* card you have been using. Whatever you do, be sure that you get a rate that you can lock into for at least a year. Make a date on your calendar to remind you when the interest rate may change; you don't want to discover that rather than paying 8 percent you are now paying 18 percent. From another student:

> *I racked up about 8k in hospital bills and credit card debt from the time I was at LSU until well into 2005. I finally had to go through bankruptcy at 25 because I didn't have any other choice. Now I am 34 with a 3k limit on my credit cards and trying desperately not to go back in debt by proudly keeping my max credit limit low.*

It is better to keep one credit card that you pay faithfully, because within the next five years you will want to finance something, whether it is a car, or an education, or a downpayment on an apartment. That card can help you because it will be used to determine your credit rating. Recently, a former student of mine who graduated this past year wanted to rent an apartment. He had a job and a credit card and his room-mate was a very well paid person in the business world. The owner of the apartment demanded that they show not only one, but *three* credit cards between them, as proof of solvency. Fortunately, the owner backed down, but such cases are probably more and more likely to occur. Nonetheless, for an actor, one card is the safest way to travel.

Necessary and expected expenses: the cost of doing business

In the first year of your career, you will have some large expenditures that you didn't have in the past. Here is where relatives can help.

Even if you don't have any rich rels (I didn't) there is probably one person who might be able to pay for your photographer, for printing your pictures, or for some audition wardrobe. Christmas is always around the corner!

Professional headshots: between $125 and $1,000

The range of prices depends on the city in which a photographer operates as well as their reputation and skill. It is extremely important that you get your professional pictures in the place where you are going to settle, from a photographer who understands the market in that area. I will discuss this in depth in the chapter on headshots and résumés.

Printing of headshots, per 100: from $50 to $300

This cost depends on quality, locale, and whether the printer is also responsible for getting rid of the pimple you got the day you had your pictures done. Because of the digital age, you really don't need to print more than 100 or so and you can always get more if you run out.

Retouching

This is done using an hourly fee. Therefore it depends on the needs of the particular job. It might be as low as $20 or as high as $200. Usually the people who do your photo reproduction do this. If not, your photographer can probably suggest a good service to you.

Union initiation fees: SAG-AFTRA, about $3,000

SAG-AFTRA (www.SAG-AFTRA.com) is the union whose jurisdiction includes film, TV, radio, and other media. It is responsible for protecting your rights on the set and ensuring that you are paid whatever you are owed. The initiation fee is about $3,000 depending on your location when you join. You can elect to pay this fee all at once (advised) or you can use a payment plan that SAG has set up through their credit union. The rate that you pay per month for this privilege has to do with—you guessed it—your credit rating!

It is very likely that your first professional SAG-AFTRA job will be a commercial. In general (and this is very general), if you were to shoot a commercial meant for broadcast TV on one day, you would receive about $600 for that day. However, this means an eight-hour day. After the standard eight hours, you would receive time and a half, which translates to $150 per hour for the next two hours, and if the session went beyond those ten hours you would receive double time, or $300 per hour. Additionally, you would receive a fee for any wardrobe you provided, and for any fitting that you attended if it were not on the day of the shoot. It is entirely possible that you would make over $900 for that day. The session fee only includes the day's labor. It doesn't include such things as holding fees, or residuals, or other potential usages. Wow! Doesn't that sound great! However, there are many other contracts that pay much less for a session and have no residual, depending on the projected use of the film or video. Contracts, even ones like these that are already agreed upon by the union, are never predictable.

My suggestion is that you NEVER spend this money until you use it to join the union. You do NOT want to be caught without the resources when you most need them. Ask someone you know who is trustworthy. Perhaps those aunts, and uncles, and grandparents, who can't help out financially, can at least hold the money for you. Don't you even think of using it. If not, you will have to take out a loan to pay the union.

SAG-AFTRA: paying your initiation fee

Eligible SAG-AFTRA performers can apply for low interest rate initiation fee loans when joining the Union. The SAG-AFTRA initiation fee loan from the member-owned SAG-AFTRA Federal Credit Union lets you make up to twenty-four monthly payments with interest rates discounted at 5% from standard credit union loan rates. You can also get an additional 5% discount when you set up an automatic monthly payment from a credit union account. On a loan amount of $3,099.00 with a fixed rate and twenty-four-month term based on creditworthiness (including automatic payment discount), payment amounts will be:

$142.18/month with 9.40% APR fixed (A credit rating)
$145.78/month with 11.90% APR fixed (B credit rating)
$150.17/month with 14.90% APR fixed (C credit rating)

A SAG-AFTRA initiation fee loan is also available to current members who are assessed at a different initiation fee. This may be due to working in an area where the initiation fee is higher than the amount previously paid, as described on the back of the SAG-AFTRA membership application. So, if you paid $3,000 for your SAG card in Minneapolis and the same card cost $3,500 in Los Angeles, you may be responsible for the difference.

Actor's Equity, AEA: $1,100

Actor's Equity (**www.actorsequity.org**) is the union that protects actors who work on stage. For most actors, getting an Equity card is the ultimate symbol of professional standing and accomplishment. Even so, it is advisable for young actors to wait to join until they have done some non-union work in the area where they reside. Once you are a union member, it is difficult to revert to non-union status.

There are several ways to get an Equity card. The first is to accumulate weeks as an "Equity Membership Candidate" or EMC. In order to do so, you need to apply when you have a job at an Equity theatre, and pay $100 to enroll in the EMC program. You will be able to become a full member after fifty weeks of employment with Equity theatres. At that time you will need to pay $400 up front and finish paying off the remaining $600 over a two-year period. As an EMC, you are not restricted in doing non-union work.

The second way to get your AEA card is to join as a member of a "sister union." You are allowed to do this if you have been a member of another performer's union, SAG-AFTRA, or AGMA, or AGVA, for a year or more. The third is to be asked to join by a theatre, because it needs to hire you for a role that is restricted to a union member by contract. Regardless of the way in which you join, the cost is $1,100. The good news is that you have two years to pay it off, interest free, once you have paid a lump sum of $400.

Miscellaneous wardrobe: $200 or so

Because your wardrobe has been the usual jeans, t-shirts, joggers, flip-flops, and sweatshirts that most student actors wear, it may come as a shock to your pocketbook when you need to dress differently. You may have to purchase several outfits better suited for stage, film, and commercials.

For film and commercials, making these choices is easy. Look at what people in your general age bracket wear in commercials, go to a thrift shop, or a consignment shop, and buy a few outfits (I never like to pay retail). Or if you can't figure out where you fit in commercial land (if you do), ask a friend to watch TV with you, make a plan together, and then the two of you should boogie on down to the store.

Commercials are all about grooming. Your clothes must be clean, not overly patterned, and well-fitting. The color should flatter your skin (wearing white on camera is usually discouraged because it can mess with the balance of the camera).

For men, one pair of black slacks, one pair of khaki pants, a blue button-down oxford shirt, a heavy silk shirt that can be worn outside of your slacks, a great looking V-neck that can be worn either alone or with a shirt underneath, a neutral sports coat, and a plain red or blue tie should be sufficient. I am assuming that your wardrobe already includes enough jeans and t-shirts and a jean jacket or other casual jacket. Unless you are older or suspect that you will be playing lots of bankers, a suit is not really needed. You should have a pair of black shoes to go with these outfits.

For women, clothing for commercials is more particular. First, do not wear skirts that are shorter than two inches above your knees unless such a skirt is requested. Second, at least for commercials, tight clothes that are fashionable currently shouldn't be quite as tight as the latest trends. Because you are a female, it is likely that you already have a party wardrobe in addition to the clothes you wear to school. But, you may not own the kinds of clothes seen in advertising. At minimum, women would do well to buy the following: a slim but not tight black skirt, another skirt, whatever style, in a solid color, several tops, some silk, some cotton, none too low-cut, no white, but colors that look good on you on camera, a blazer or jacket of some sort, a cardigan in a neutral color, a little black dress, a pair of black pumps no more than two inches in the heel and simple jewelry. Keep these things clean and pressed, you may need them at a moment's notice.

Film auditions may require other sorts of clothing. If you need something extraordinary for film, your agent will tell you, but with your current wardrobe and the commercial wardrobe, you should be fine.

Wardrobe for theatre should be clothes that show your body, that flatter you, that you can move in, and that aren't too trendy. You're looking for neutral but attractive. Bright colors and whites are okay here. Don't wear shoes or jewelry that call attention to themselves.

Grooming beyond college: hair, between $40 and $125

People in show business need versatile hair that is not too trendy and that looks healthy and well cut. For men, it is no longer possible to just let your hair grow long or to shave it all off. Get a good cut from a stylist who knows how to shape a cut. If you don't know how to find a stylist, ask your agent, or someone you know who has great hair and seems to know how to maintain it. Women need to be sure that their hair doesn't overshadow their faces, that their bangs don't cover their eyes, and if they want to wear it long, they must know how to put it up.

Transportation

If you have relied on buses or trains to get to school with a student discount card, you will need to buy full fare cards now.

Relocation: rent, utilities, car, etc.

It is usual for students to relocate within three years of leaving school. This may simply be a move to another neighborhood, or it may mean a move across country. Before you make any moves, it is a good idea to find out what the going cost of housing is in the area to which you are moving. Also, when doing so, don't neglect the cost of utilities associated with a new location. Depending on where you move, such things can be far more expensive that you might be used to paying.

If you are moving to a city with a good public transportation system like Chicago, Boston, New York, Atlanta, or Washington, DC, it is best to rely on it, if that is at all possible. However, if you can't use public transportation, try to calculate not only the cost of the car and insurance, but also the mileage, parking, and cost of fuel in your chosen area.

Health insurance

If you are under 26, it is possible that you are still insured under your parents' insurance plans. However, there are many of you who are not covered in this way. As a young person you might believe that you won't get sick, but it is entirely possible that you could be hit by a car, fall off a stage, or break an arm playing basketball. It is unlikely that your day job will include health insurance, so it is a good idea for you to purchase health insurance through the Affordable Care website (**www.healthcare.gov**). Don't misunderstand this new set of laws. The government is not selling insurance; it simply gives you a list of insurance companies that feature good value for your money. The price of such a policy is based on your income. Failure to have health insurance might mean that you will incur a fine. Much more importantly, without insurance, you may be hit with medical expenses far beyond your ability to pay, and at that time the government will not come to your rescue. I am not telling you that you must buy insurance, I am telling you that failing to do so could destroy your life for quite some time to come.

All of these financial obstacles will figure into the five-year plan for your Life Play. It is now time to make a plan of attack to overcome your artistic obstacles, and to live your life (at least for the next five years) as successfully as possible.

6

Access to the Fulfillment of Your Life Play

In chapters 4 and 5 you examined your dreams and the obstacles to them. You made a schedule and projected when and how you might overcome many obstacles. Take a bow (applause heard offstage) even if you have only done half of it.

After all your work, it is finally time to begin gaining access to people who can help! The biggest problem for a young actor is getting into the hearts, minds, and memories of the folks that can hire you or help you to be hired. This is like any experience where you are seen as a stranger or as an underling. When you first entered high school, you probably had to work to find people who would not shun you for being a freshman. There were also new people in your own freshman class to be met. Who were you going to hang with? What friends should and would you make? Would you isolate and keep your junior-high friends, or would you risk reaching out and expanding your horizons? How frightened and how hopeful were you? Some of you may have decided that in high school you would change everything about yourself. Some of you may have decided to become the hardest working kid in school, or the star of the theatre group, or the president of the student body. You may not have planned any of this on paper but you had some sort of theory about how to make it in high school.

If you stop to think about it, all of the success you wanted or needed depended on other people—on keeping and growing relationships. The first of these were not your teachers, they were fellow students. You needed to gain access to them, and you did it by trying to be a friend, by being loyal, by being reliable, and by being good at what you thought they valued. You probably did a lot of observation about how the high school game worked, and tried as hard as you could to adapt to it, or to rebel against it, depending on your own set of values and loneliness. You learned new ways of dressing, walking, talking, and you learned the rules involving what to say, who was in the crowd you wanted to join, and who wasn't. You did all of this to gain access to high school success.

Entering the theatrical school of hard knocks is exactly the same. Over the first several years you are enrolled, it can be both frustrating and depressing. If you hang in there you will probably figure out the rules of the game just as you tried to do back as a high school freshman. *If you pay attention*, you will succeed.

The problem in show business is that the rules are even less obvious than those in high school, and you will trip and fall many times. You will need friends! They may actually be more important to you in the long run than professional contacts.

There are lots of ways to gain access to people you want to hang with in your career—the actors, writers, and directors in the city of your choice. You can usually accomplish this by attending auditions where you will meet others in your metaphoric freshman class. Don't run from these without ever having met anyone—you will miss very important relationships. Suggest having coffee or drinks and understand that *these folks are not your competition; they are your comrades* in the battle for access. Perhaps you will meet friends in an acting class at the professional studio you decide to attend. Again, work to create a group of like-minded and hardworking people who can back each other up when times get rough. Having such a group of friends, all in the same boat, is a great way to stay afloat.

If there is a theatre you want to work with, volunteer to do *anything*, anything at all, from ushering to cleaning up after the show. Just as in high school, you need to get your face and your name out there. Someone will finally notice you if you are reliable, and if you do a good job. That can lead to many things, auditions and readings among them.

Another way to become a part of the actor clique is by attending every audition possible in your first year out of school. You will meet tons of people and get lots of advice, some of it good, some bad, but you will meet *all ages and kinds* of people. Don't neglect people older than you, they have been through it! In attending these auditions, your audition skills will grow so that when you really need them, they will be sharp.

However—a slight warning about the "audition for everything" idea. If you have planned well, there will be writers and companies and directors you have identified with whom you want to work. But there will also be those who will be of no use at all on your résumé. Before you go to the audition, take a look at the reviews they have gotten in the last several years, and then decide what to do. Some directors and some theatre companies are known for bad work; find this out before committing to them.

Why would this matter if you only planned to audition? Because you may be asked to do shows at theatres where you have no desire to work, or with directors or companies whom you would rather avoid. The danger lies in the fact that you are an actor and (come on, admit it) easily flattered. All actors want to be invited to do a show; just an invitation is a great lift to the ego. If you are called back, you will feel wonderful, and sadly, on the spur of the moment, you may decide to do a show that you will live to regret.

So, go to as many auditions as you can, and if you are called back, know ahead of time whether you want to commit or not. You may also decide as a result of the disorganization or rudeness of a director, or a casting director, that the place you thought was so cool is not a happy place. It is fine to audition, but very bad etiquette to attend a callback unless you intend to accept a part if it is offered. Your loyalty to the project will be assumed if you take the callback. It is not hard to turn down a callback, simply say that you are doing another show, or that you have new work hours or something of the kind. The theatre world can be as cliquish as high school so, yes, I am suggesting some fibs here; you don't want to insult them by saying you don't want to work with them after they have gotten excited about you.

So far, I have addressed the need to connect to a pod of theatre people like yourself. We all need lots of support in the early days, but, another warning, be very careful to avoid complainers, cynics, and negative people who do very little to advance their careers. They will talk forever about what a b-tch a certain agent is, or what a bad director so and so is, or how a particular casting director doesn't "like" them, or how awful another actor's performance is in a show they are doing. These are not professional manners and such attitudes are contagious. It is tempting to fall in with poisonous people; they can make you feel good because they find excuses for why failure happens. However, as David Mamet says, "Action talks, bullshit walks."

If you yourself are given to these sorts of messages and thoughts, if you are tempted to downgrade the people around you, if you feel competitive with your fellow actors, take a good look at the fears and insecurities that lead you to such destructive behavior. You must overcome them or they will overcome you. Find a support group to help lift you out of your negative morass. If such a group doesn't appeal to you, meditation can be a lifesaver. Another method of getting rid of these dangerous thoughts is writing them out fully every morning and casting them into the garbage so that you can start the day clean. Sometimes writing like this can help you to see in black and white how petty and unfounded your angers and fears actually are.

Frequently, a bad attitude is based on the feeling that the world is centered around you, and that other people pay attention to you more than they actually do. In actuality, we rarely pay attention to people who don't help us to achieve our dreams. Face it, we are the main character in our own lives and people who can't be of aid or comfort, or with whom we have little contact, are simply extras. It is a sort of reverse egotism to believe that a certain casting person, or director, or agent dislikes you. This implies that you have some importance to them. Alas, probably not. Unless you have acted like a complete a-hole, they don't even remember you. If you have acted like a complete a-hole, then you must accept the fact that they may not want to work with you for a while. It is rare that anyone, regardless of how badly they have behaved, will be banished for life.

Mental hygiene is as important as brushing your teeth: find a way to prevent cavities and being an a-hole! I have known and taught many very unpleasant, though talented, actors; their road is not an easy one. The business can make anyone behave atrociously, but if you begin in that way, you may never even have a chance to discover that fact.

Other than friends, the most necessary relationships you need to establish are those that you probably most fear— the casting directors and agents who seem to hold the keys to your every dream. In reality, they can only give you access, they can't get a job for you, and they can't make you a better actor. Regardless of what you may have been told, they are helpers. They are invested in your success; they can only win when you do. They may be very distant, sheltered behind secretaries, interns, assistants, and associates. They set up these walls to discourage amateurs. They really do expect you to work so hard that they will be forced to open a door in the wall because of your value. By working hard, I don't mean making a pest of yourself. I *do* mean that you must not be discouraged when they don't open the door and run out to greet you with open arms. As a matter of fact, if they do, you might want to be a little suspicious. How successful are they if they have the time to devote to newbies like you? In cities other than LA and New York, you will probably get a cordial welcome—the walls are not very tall and there are lots of doors—but in the Big Apple and the Big Orange, they are fortresses. It is also important to remember that the world is rarely ever (so far as I can tell) fair.

If your dream is to move to LA/NYC, it is best for you to learn the ropes in cities where you can fail and fail again, fall down and get up, and the doors will still be open. In the smaller markets, you will learn quite a bit because the business itself doesn't differ all that much except in style and scale. These lessons will help you to gain access in LA/NYC (if you must go there) more quickly than if you moved directly after graduation. You will be able to get your union cards far more easily in regional markets, you may be able to get some film on yourself for a reel, you will become better at auditioning, and perhaps your agent will be able to connect you with a colleague in the big markets.

Moving to LA/NYC without union affiliations, representation, and/ or experience beyond school is a really bad idea because gaining access there will take you twice as long. Take some time to become familiar with the professional world in a place where your ignorance is not disdained. Think about how many star-struck people with no training and less talent move to LA/NYC every day. They may indeed be the next mega-star, but usually they are simply the next waiter at the local coffee shop. The profession usually disregards these folks, but because of the vast numbers of them, it is difficult for actors to separate themselves.

Contacting agents and casting directors

It is a ritual of passage for actors to send out headshots, résumés, and brief letters in big manila envelopes to agents and casting people when they graduate or decide they have studied long enough. If you feel compelled to do this, go ahead, it might get you seen, or maybe not. When these manila envelopes arrive in the mail, an agent or a casting person rarely opens them. This duty is usually assigned to an intern or assistant. These hope-filled envelopes sit in stacks for a week or a month in some corner of the office until someone has the time to open them. They are then put in another stack of things for the agent or casting director to look at when there's a spare moment. At that time, the agent or director will go through and put the interesting ones, or the ones that have credits or education that can't be ignored, in a pile of "see when we have time." The rest are thrown away.

Perhaps it would be better to simply send an introductory letter with your picture on it along with a résumé by snail mail. If the body of the letter contains something useful or charming for the agent or casting person, you may be contacted.

However, the best way to meet is by recommendation from a friend, a teacher, a casting director, or a director. This may be a phone call made on your behalf, or perhaps your friend will walk you into their own agency and introduce you. *Being given this sort of help is precious and invaluable.* Do not use such a favor to simply "feel out" the market unless the people who are helping you know that's what you're doing. Time is precious to talent buyers and sellers, and seeing people who won't be of use is not a good way to spend it. For the person doing the recommendation, there are only a certain number of favors that any of us can ask of our busy colleagues in agentry or casting before we become annoying. As a teacher, I don't recommend anyone who won't take the introduction seriously. If an actor I have suggested fails to show up, or shows up in an unprofessional manner, or constantly tries to change the appointment time, I look bad. I have lost one of the favors in my wallet that might have been spent on a more deserving actor.

This happened to me recently when I suggested an actor for a role to a casting director who had called to ask if I had any students who might be right for a movie she was casting. I said that I had just seen a young man deliver a terrific performance in a show at the university. School was almost over and he would be free to shoot the movie. I immediately called him (I'll name him Larry) and told him to contact the casting director by phone; she was expecting his call that afternoon. As it happens, Larry waited and called too late in the day to reach her. He left a message and she tried to contact him by phone and by email the next day. After two days, she called me to ask whether he was actually flaky or simply ignorant. He now had two red marks next to his name from her perspective, and my stock was falling. I contacted him again and, for one reason or another, he still didn't act immediately. He didn't actually contact the casting director until a day later, and he never responded to the emails that were sent to him. Unfortunately, young people seem to respond to text messaging but the business uses email, and perhaps that was the problem. These things happen very, very quickly. I made excuses for him, but he had damaged his reputation (and mine) because he neither recognized the value of the introduction when it was made, nor the need to jump on the opportunity that presented itself. Your reputation is the most important thing that you have. As a new person in the business, you are given some mercy, as he will be, but there aren't that many chances.

If you happen to get an introduction to a potential talent buyer, do not wait or hesitate, the gift has a short life span. And, do not ask for an introduction unless you are actually going to be available in the city for the next six months or so. In my casting life, I met lots of actors who disappeared by the time I called them for an audition—a waste of time and effort for both of us.

Larry's story is not unusual. Actors have an almost genetic tendency towards self-sabotage. Los Angeles casting director Tammy Billik commented that for her the worst form of self-sabotage was appearing to be too cocky. "Confidence is good. Cockiness can knock out a young actor." Again, a-holedom, even if it is an unfortunate defense mechanism, is a problem. There are many other forms of self-sabotage guaranteed to keep you from the danger of actually working. As Mickie Paskal, a Chicago casting director, says:

I would say, on average, fifty percent of the talent that I see on a daily basis engages in some form of self-sabotage, whether it be a lack of preparation, an attitude of disinterest, a lack of availability or some form of professionally inappropriate behavior. It is rampant. It is absolutely understandable, the rejection is infinitely more easily handled if the actor can convince him or herself that they didn't fully risk the preparation that may have landed them the role. I think it is easier to face the rejection mentally if they know they didn't give it one hundred percent. I try to remind actors all the time that there is GLORY in the risking of preparation. That it will always pay off— maybe not in the short term, but definitely throughout their careers.

Here are some other forms of self-sabotage, all taken from real-life experience:

- Being late.
- Not working on the sides or copy.
- Not reading the play/screenplay if it is available.
- Not dressing appropriately.
- Bringing your bad mood into the casting room.
- Bringing lots of props to use.
- Wearing strong perfume.
- Bringing your pet along.
- Being defensive in the audition when asked to make adjustments.
- Not filling out the appropriate paperwork.
- Cursing your agent in the lobby, loudly, when the sides or copy you got from them was wrong.
- Having liquor on your breath.
- Passing out clever self-promotional materials to the auditors.
- Shaking hands with everyone in the room.
- Telling the director that the casting director who is present in the room didn't tell them anything about the role.
- Being unaware that most auditions, somehow, screw up despite everyone's best efforts.

Please, please be aware of the insidious problem of stupidity caused by the desire to act. Agents and casting people know all about it because it is so prevalent. When I was casting, there were times when I felt that actors were simply addicted to failure. They acted as if they had lost all common sense and civility when dealing with us. New interns would remark on how weird the actors were, and I would just shrug and say, "They're actors, that is how they are, forgive them and get used to it." Those same interns went on to cast nationally and internationally and to become heads of talent agencies. You must be sure that when you interact with anyone from the business you do so knowing the stakes. Manners and kindness are essential aspects of the business for actors even when the business is rude and dismissive of them. Your ability to behave well in rehearsals or on a shoot is judged by how you interact with the casting offices and the agents with whom you come into contact.

Taking a class with a casting director, an agent, or a director is another way to access the buyers and sellers in the business. I strongly suggest that if you do so, you spend your money on the people in your vicinity from whom you might legitimately expect to receive an audition as well as from whom you can actually learn something. At the present time, there are a number of casting directors offering classes in LA and some in New York. In those cities, it has become common knowledge that many of these "classes" are payments to the casting directors to do what they should be doing for free as a major part of their profession. The scams are outrageous and I suspect that the unions will step in sooner or later. If you decide to pay to be seen by a casting director, at least know what you're doing—as John Patrick Shanley says, "experience the lie."

If you don't live in LA/NYC do not expect that a casting director from either of those markets offering classes in your city will remember you, or take you home with them, or call you in for an audition. These people travel and teach to make money, pure and simple. There are so many scam artists out there who prey on people who want to believe there is an easy way to "make it" in films. These criminals appeal to uneducated and deluded people who desperately want there to be magic. There isn't any magic, there aren't any shortcuts, there aren't secret ways known only to a few.

How will you recognize rip-offs? The signs are: a very high-priced class, an overly short class, a very large class, a promise of work as a result of taking the class, lots of splashy advertising, and/or a lack of requirements to be admitted to the class. These small-time crooks will often tell their victims, in person and on websites, that there is a shortage of talent, and that Hollywood is looking for actors all the time. They may be pushing poor wannabes to pay large amounts to be included in some big publication or webpage that they claim everyone uses. They may tell their victims to have pictures done by their favorite photographer who just happens to be available, and who just happens to be in their employ. Believe me, there are so many actors and near-actors and non-actors and beauty contest winners working hard every day in NYC and LA and Chicago and Miami and Seattle and everywhere in between, that there is no shortage of people from whom to cast. Don't be a dummy—before taking a class check out the credentials of the people involved. If he or she has cast only cartoons, music videos, or reality TV, they will probably not be able to help you acquire on-camera skills for film or television. You can research just about anyone at **www.IMDB.com**. Even if you are not affiliated, you can call an agent or a casting director's office and ask about the merits of the person advertising a class.

There are many casting directors in your own cities who teach, and because such local knowledge is valuable, it might be wiser to study with them. Just remember, go to learn, not to impress. And there are some really wonderful teachers out there, so don't reject the idea of studying with a casting director out of hand. Before I became a casting director, I was an acting teacher; I only started casting because my students weren't being given access. Thank God I returned to my senses and the classroom! I know many casting people who are really magnificent teachers. It stands to reason that after watching so many actors, both good and bad, they have an innate understanding of what needs to be done. If you can't determine, you should ask your agent who should have some understanding of the quality of the teacher and the class. If you do take a class with a casting director or agent, be aware that you will learn quite a lot, but also be aware that you must work at the top of your game and treat everyone with respect. There have been times in my teaching life when I have brought professionals to class to see students do monologues or scenes, and many of the students thought that, because it was a class, it wasn't business. *Whenever* you meet anyone from the business, in *whatever* capacity— it's business. Never ever forget it.

I am reminded of a young lady in my audition class who was lucky enough to present a monologue to a very important agent. The agent, who was visiting on his own time, responded to her monologue presentation by saying that he felt she needed to make a stronger choice of monologue material. She looked right at him and said, "That's not what the guy last week told me." There are so many kinds of wrong in her response that I can't even list them.

Chicago casting director Mickie Paskal tells of visiting an on-camera class where a young person in the front row appeared not only bored but also hostile, and whose cynicism shone through all of the questions and the work that followed. I find it absurd that an actor who hasn't even entered a career should be cynical, but I do know that cynicism is a defense against disappointment and fear. If you are bored, hostile, and cynical, recall that you are an actor and capable of appearing to be interested, warm, and trusting!

The best way to meet an agent, a casting director, or a director is to be good in a show! But, depending on how many productions are going on in your city, it is often difficult for talent buyers to see everything. Most of them do try to know what's going on in their area. Send a postcard or a letter inviting them to your show along with an offer of complimentary tickets and a way to reserve a seat. (It may not be a bad investment to offer tickets even if you must pay for them.) Be aware that industry people don't like to leave the city limits, so choose your shows carefully. Whether or not these folks actually attend a performance, send them reviews (if you are mentioned favorably). If your work is good, the agent, casting director, or director will eventually take notice. You don't actually determine when your dues in the business have been paid, but you will know when they have been because you will be welcomed into the club.

I have not discussed postcards or letters in any depth as of yet. Postcards in particular are great marketing devices because they're cheap, sometimes they end up on the addressee's desk, and you can put your headshot and agency contact info on one side and a note on the other. The note can be anything from:

Hey, I just got cast as Stella in *Streetcar* at Acme Theatre, we open Dec 1, 2015 and I am excited. Thanks to my agent at Brown Street Agency for making this possible

to

Inviting you to see *Streetcar* at Acme Theatre, directed by Alice Gilbert, comps are waiting, call 333 333 3333. We play Tues through Sun from October 6 to Nov 22

or simply

Merry Christmas!

These cards function as brand identification, just like product placement in a film or the repetition of Coca-Cola signs all over the world. If you are diligent and mail these out frequently, by the end of the year many of the people you want to reach will know your name and face. While the adage goes that "it's who you know," it might be wiser to say, "it's who knows you."

If your first contact with the business is the big manila envelopes, your next postal adventure should be the aforementioned mail in envelopes with stamps. These letters can vary from simple introductions to "query" letters, so named because they are sent to inquire about something.

An introductory letter should be well crafted and pointed at a particular theatre, casting director, or agency. Generally, such a letter is not sent to a director. As with everything you send, your picture should appear on your stationery along with your contact information. Something to remember is that the best letter reveals how you might help the person to whom you are writing solve a problem. This letter should not be a direct request for work; it should help the intended agent or casting director or company manager understand why you might be a good future candidate for them.

This missive should be specific and you might want to do some research concerning who you are writing to. It must not be a form letter nor overly formal. As with all letters, leading the first paragraph with "I" is considered bad form. Bad spelling is disrespectful, and looks as if you aren't paying attention. (I know there are many of you who can't spell, and I know how silly the rules of spelling are, but none of that makes any difference, you must rely on spellcheck, or a dictionary, or your former English major roommate who is a whiz at such things.) As an aside, I have seen actors whose résumés contain misspellings of the names of the shows they were in, the characters they played, and even the names of the directors for whom they have worked. Such carelessness leads some of us to worry that either you can't concentrate, that you are lazy, or that you are one of the many narcissists in the acting population. It announces to the world that you are not professional yet. So too, any letters you write must be formatted and spelled correctly.

The best of these letters will include:

- Why you are writing to that person specifically.

- How you might be helpful to that person's agency or projects.

- If you have met the person to whom you are writing, a reminder of when and where that took place.

- Information about your current situation: are you doing a show, just graduating, getting married, what?

- Some compliment about them or their work. If you are writing to someone about whom you have no enthusiasm, don't write until you do.

Following are examples of good query letters.

Example: Agent Query Letter

Colin Sphar

actorcolin@someemail.com

(223) 554 5023

Hi Jess,   June 10, 2016

We met in March when you visited the DePaul audition class. I've been busy this past month with the showcase, graduation and a two-week trip to Italy! And now I'm ready to get to work in this business of acting.

I just shot my first commercial last week and am interested in getting more involved with film, television and commercials. I have heard your agency spoken well of from several sources. I feel I would be a good fit for Grossman & Jack because of my training, look and ability to crossover into voiceover and print.

I remember having a good interaction with you the little time we were in the room together at DePaul. I'd like to speak with you further and show you some more of my range. I'm a versatile actor with comedic as well as dramatic ability. I hope we can meet soon!

Peace,
Colin Sphar

Example: Theatre Casting Director General Query Letter

Note that this young actor's letter is conversational and doesn't feel academic or corporate.

Sean Parris

SParris@someemail.com

Blankney Agency

211-916-0627

Dear Timothy,   July 3, 2017

We met at your introduction to the Remy Bumppo Theatre Company at the Greenhouse Performing Space a couple of months ago, and I saw you again in May at DePaul's Theatre School Showcase. (I did a piece from Henry V.)

Remy Bumppo is one of the theatre companies that I want to work with because of my love for heightened language and passion for the clash of ideas in classical writing. I was excited to hear you express your interest in addressing the relevance of Shakespeare to contemporary life. As an African American actor, I believe that the classics frequently speak far louder than plays fresh off the printing presses. I would love to audition for you this year. I look forward to Remy Bumppo's growth under your leadership.

Sincerely,
Sean Parris

Example: Less Formatted Letter, But Still A Good One

Michael McKeogh

211-916-0627

Mckeo@someemail.com

May 25, 2017

To the Attention of the Casting Office of Rough Players Theatre,

(The actor in this case should have found out the casting director's name before sending the letter.)

Hello!

My name is Michael McKeogh and I will be graduating with an MFA in Acting from The Theatre School at DePaul University. After I return from the Showcase in June, I plan on staying in Chicago. Joan Eggers recently came to our class and gave a talk about the formation of the Rough Players company that I found both fascinating and inspiring. She also spoke a little bit about her musical *Howl* that made me excited to see the production. I have worked with the director, Johnny Mayberry, on his children's show *Make Mine Strawberry*. I found working with him a pleasure. I am drawn to your company and the passion with which you work.

I noticed you are doing a show about the great Chicago fire, which I find intriguing, my undergraduate degree was in Urban Planning and I wrote my thesis on the reconstruction of Chicago following the fire. Attached is my headshot and resume. I would love a chance to come in and read. Thank you very much!

Sincerely,
Michael McKeogh

Example: Query Letter to Director Regarding a Specific Show
Note: This actress writes very personally to the director of this show, and it doesn't hurt that she compliments her as well. She also includes a little humor without seeming to be working too hard.

Alissa Walker

Alissa2@someemail.com

(769) 374 7643
Blankey Management
(554) 596 2468

Dear Karen,   JULY 23, 2017

It is exciting to hear that you are going to be directing Ellen Clay's new play *A Walk with Strangers*. I saw the last show of hers that you directed and was blown away. After seeing it, I read everything she has written and found out that she and I are from the same hometown. It makes sense that her writing speaks to me more than any other contemporary playwright, we have both walked the same old tree lined streets. I would love to audition for the show.

If already cast, or if you don't see me in any of the roles, I would be pleased to help you in any way that I can. I have done some assistant directing, and I am very good at getting coffee, taking notes, and cleaning up after people leave!

I am enclosing my resume in this note and if you turn this letter over, you will find my resume. We must always conserve paper.

Regards,
Alissa Walker

7

The Cast of Your Life Play:

Casting Directors, Agents, and Managers: Who They Are and What They Do

Casting directors

I worked as a freelance casting director for many years, and was lucky enough to receive an award from the Casting Society of America for my work on the film, *Fargo*. Because I was a casting director in the Midwest, my title for films was usually "Location Casting Director" and I made my living casting not only film, but also TV series (*The Women of Brewster Place*). I was hired at times to search for one role or several roles in films and series being cast elsewhere, and to provide a substantial amount of actors for projects being shot in the Midwest. This type of casting is called *theatrical casting*, whether location casting or not. The term, theatrical casting, refers to film and television casting, not to stage or commercials.

When I cast commercials, I was called a "Commercial Casting Director," and when I was asked to find not only actors, but "real people" I was referred to as a "Street" or "Real People Casting Director." Additionally, I was hired to find various roles for various theatres including the Tyrone Guthrie Theater and the Actors' Theatre of Louisville. That type of casting is often referred to as *legit* casting because it is for the legitimate stage. I was a "Full Service Casting Director!"

When I encounter actors and members of the public, I often need to explain what it is that casting directors do and what they don't do. *The first thing to say is what we don't do—we don't select the cast*. Only a director can do that. Casting directors are hired because of their taste, expertise with actors, knowledge of actors in their vicinity, their ability to understand the kind of actor a given script needs and their knowledge of the director's taste and vision. The casting director's actual job is to present a short menu of the best actors available in their geographical area to the director and/or the producer and/or the advertising company and/or the studio. In this chapter I have created several charts to help visualize the different ways in which casting is done depending on the media involved. Take note of the actor's position in all of this.

Film casting

Casting people are a part of what is called *pre-production* or "pre-pro," which means anything done before full production begins. It is rare for most film casting directors to be in rehearsal or on the set because they are usually busy working on their next job. People always ask me whether I liked working with Bill Murray on *Groundhog Day* or with Bill Macy on *Fargo*, but I never met either of them. Bill was hired to do *Groundhog Day* long before I was hired. The film wouldn't have gotten financing without his name and the name of Andie McDowell, both of whom were stars at the time and therefore very bankable. That is how the business usually works—money people don't like taking a chance on a movie without a star or two attached to it. So, it is possible that the main title casting director will not have met the stars before they are cast either.

Most film casting directors are freelancers who are hired for the week, the day, or until the completion of the casting for a given project. Their jobs and reputations depend on the quality and appropriateness of the actors they present to the director. Outside of Los Angeles, freelancers maintain their own offices while their colleagues in LA usually have office space with the production companies with whom they work. In New York, theatrical casting directors may or may not maintain offices, and they may also do more television casting than their more specialized LA colleagues.

Regardless of what they do or where they are located, good casting directors know what is going on in their city, what actors are coming up, and how best the actors they know can be used. They see everything they can, read reviews, meet as many actors as time permits, and study the directors with whom they work. It is entirely possible that you will meet a casting director before you ever have an agent. Casting directors are always looking for the unfound actors to add to their secret casting possibilities. We pride ourselves on being on top of our markets.

Do not make the mistake of calling us casting *agents*—we have fought long and hard to achieve the title of casting director, because, in essence, we direct the casting. Unlike agents, we are paid by and allied to a project, or to an advertising company, or to a production company. Agents are talent sellers and are paid by the actors they represent. It is possible that the mix-up between casting directors and agents is due to the fact that the office where the casting director works is called a casting agency. And to add to that confusion, agents will sometimes tape actors themselves to submit for projects when a local casting director has not been brought onto the job.

A word to the wise—do not forget the casting director's names, nor what they do. You expect them to remember you, and so you must remember them. They do not need to be sent gifts, nor should actors be subservient; casting directors depend as much on actors as actors depend on them. The best way of thinking of them all—casting directors, agents, and managers, is that you are all business friends and colleagues, each working to do your jobs to the best of your abilities.

Just like agents, casting directors exist everywhere: in LA, NYC, Chicago, Minneapolis, Atlanta, Houston, Dallas, Miami, Seattle, and many other metropolitan areas. In each market there may be people who specialize in one thing, or people who cast all sorts of projects. In LA/NYC, these specialties are usually not interchangeable.

Regardless of where or what is being cast, the hierarchy of casting differs depending on the medium. Here I have provided charts outlining these ways of working. However, as it turns out, the actor is always at the bottom of the process.

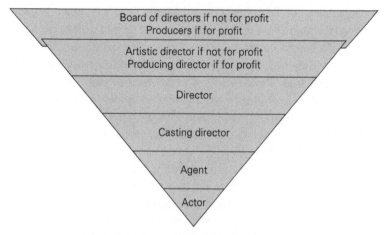

Example: hierarchy in legitimate theatre

Stage casting

The casting directors with whom you are probably most familiar are the stage or "legitimate" casting directors who are usually salaried employees on the staff of a particular theatre. These casting directors' responsibilities include planning the casting for an entire season for their theatres while keeping an eye open for new talent in the area. Often they work with an already chosen company of actors. These folks need to be expert in the "style" of their theatre, and the taste of the directors with whom they work. Often they travel to see actors outside of their own city in order to assemble a cast for a particular show.

Because they have a longer relationship with their institution, they frequently have more influence in determining which actors are hired than their counterparts in film and TV. In their daily routine, they may meet with directors to discuss casting and the script, contact agents as well as freelance actors, and of course, run auditions. Often they will give actors adjustments in the sessions before the director is present. This is done not only to see whether the actor can come closer to the vision of the director, but also to test how the actor takes direction and how flexible he or she is. Such casting directors often have great directing abilities and go on to direct and produce on their own.

Following a round of auditions, the casting director will select three or four actors to present to the director—rarely more. Once an actor is cast, the casting director will offer contracts to the chosen actors either directly or through their agents. Once the cast is set, they will usually contract with actors for understudy roles. (There are times when the understudies don't need to be seen by the director because the director trusts the casting person.) Theatre casting directors must be knowledgeable about the Actors' Equity contracts governing their particular theatre. Additionally, they may function as assistants to the director or the producer, and they may be teachers in schools within the institutions for which they work. To work at a theatre in such a way involves a great deal of political skill, artistic acumen, and ability to work regularly with a team of directors.

Mechanics of film and television casting

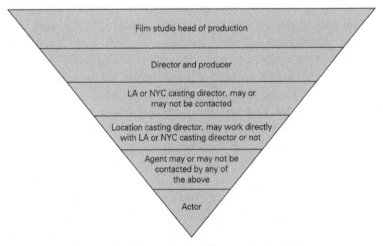

Example: hierarchy for film and television

Currently, the way the entire system of casting works in film and TV is that casting directors release a "breakdown" for the roles they are casting, either on their own or through a company called Breakdown Services. These breakdowns include descriptions of the characters as well as information about when and where the job will take place, where the audition will be, and the days scheduled for both auditions and callbacks. These breakdowns containing the "specs" (specific needs of the job) are sent to all the agents who subscribe to Breakdown Services. Depending on many variables, not all castings are released to Breakdown. It is not usual for *stage* casting directors to use Breakdown Services, although it has been known to happen. When the agents read the breakdown, they submit, usually electronically, pictures of the actors whom they wish to have considered. The submission is generally via a website called Actor's Access.

The casting director, who has undoubtedly made their own "must see" list, then reviews the submissions and alerts the agents as to which actors they wish to audition, the roles for which they want the actors to read, when and where the actors should arrive at the audition, and other information concerning wardrobe and other requirements. Along with this submission, the casting person will send the *sides* (portions of the script the actors must be prepared to do) either via e-mail, via Actor's Access, or via a private website that some casting offices maintain for such activities. In the case of a movie, if there is a full script available, by union rules it must be available in the casting office the day prior to the auditions.

Before the advent of electronic technology, this was all done on the phone and using messenger services. You have no idea what a monumental job it was and how much paper was wasted. When I first began casting, it would not be unusual for me to work from 10 a.m. to 10 p.m. to get all of the work done. There would be stacks of pictures sent by agents, often more than two feet high, to sort through, hundreds of phone calls to the agents to schedule the actors, more phone calls to determine if they were "confirmed" or to reschedule if needed, and many more phone calls to and from the producers who would be calling to change what they were looking for, or to add a few categories when the scripts changed. When faxing came into our world, it cut down on much of this hectic work, but the phones never stopped ringing with calls from agents, clients, lost actors, and people who felt that calling the casting office to ask how to break into the business would be a good idea. Like most of my casting colleagues, I was often tired and crabby.

As a location casting director, time is the enemy because more often than not the producer is in New York, while the director, or in the case of commercials, the advertising agency, is in Portland, Oregon, or Kuala Lumpur. Time zones still mean making and receiving phone calls from LA, which is two hours behind Chicago and New York, which is one hour ahead. Casting is always a hurry-up business and while I was working in Chicago we needed to get to Federal Express by 9.30 p.m. in order to send the video tapes to the various parties that we had copied at the end of a day of casting. All of this is done electronically; casting tapes are uploaded, sometimes in real time, or the auditions are done using Skype with no uploads needed. This has reduced some of the stress levels for casting people, but even in this day of cyber communications, the job demands enormous energy and stamina. It begins the minute the casting person gets out of bed and doesn't end until he or she has the guts to turn off the cellphone.

Another frustration for casting directors is that for film, and television, the availability of the director to see actors is very limited because the director has many other time commitments. In the case of a series, the casting director may simply be able to cast the smaller roles without the director meeting them, but this is not always the case. Usually, there is only time to see three actors per role and often the producer asks that this be done in a day or two. Because of this, the casting director needs to read as many actors as possible to make sure that the three actors they believe can do the role can actually do it. In addition to requesting submitted actors, the casting director is also fielding calls from the producer, deciding which scenes (sides) need to be read for the first reads and which for the second, and if the director wants to see more than one scene. Then the agents begin calling and e-mailing to discuss which actors can and cannot make the audition, who needs to reschedule, and what should the actors wear? Casting people NEED assistants!

Another problem is presented when the script is changed or rewritten. In the case of a series or a sitcom, this might occur daily, and the roles that were being sought yesterday (who the casting director has scheduled to be seen today) are no longer in the script. A re-prep is needed before the end of the day. This is also generally the case in commercials. Film is less likely to be so significantly rewritten, but the demands of the production company can be far more difficult to deal with. Producers and directors often want the casting director to read their family and friends and the waiter they met yesterday. Or, they have heard about a particular actor in a play or a film, the name of whom they can't recall, but they need to see that guy. Or, they want you to find that diamond in the rough on the streets of your town. Because the director only gets to do a film every year or two if he or she is lucky, the stakes are very high, and casting is where a movie usually makes it or breaks it.

When I was working on the movie *Fargo*, the Coen brothers had the notion that everyone in the film needed to be blond or close to it. There were a lot of really angry brunettes in Minneapolis. For two weeks, I read every blond actor and actress in the city as well as all the blond young boys who were needed to play the son of the kidnapped wife. The first boy I read was not, as he had been promised to be, blond, but I taped him anyway. He was very good. *But* he was not blond and the brothers wouldn't give in on the issue. I went back home to Chicago for a few weeks while the LA casting director tied up the roles we couldn't cast in the Midwest and secured the remaining leads for the film. He also sought a little blond boy.

A month later, I was sent back to Minneapolis to hold an open-call, I advertised on the radio and TV for the blond son of the kidnapped woman. Hundreds of adorable and not so adorable children later, the Coen brothers decided that the first boy, the brunette, was the only one who could do the role. Did they dye his hair blond? No, they did not. Somehow directors can be odd.

Commercial casting

In commercial casting, the clients want to see as many people as possible for the roles. This is a plus for actors! Because freelance casting directors outside of LA are full-service casting directors, they cast TV, film, commercials, and some stage, and therefore are able to see actors when the stakes aren't so high. Actors often think of this as a "cattle call," though that is not the case. A cattle call is a casting call so general that anyone can show up at any time. It is often done when conducting a national search and may in fact simply be a way of publicizing a project economically. Most commercial auditions are done through agents in the usual way; the casting directors have requested to see the actors they think have a shot at the commercial or taken a chance on an actor they haven't seen who is suggested by an agent.

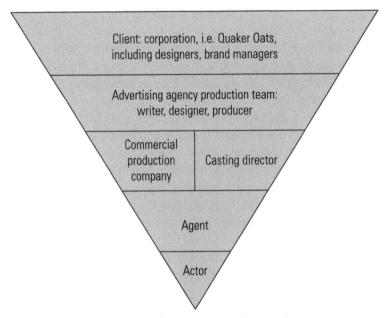

Example: hierarchy of the commercial casting process

Actors make the mistake of assuming that if the casting director whose name is on the door is not personally present at their audition they haven't been noticed by the named casting director. This is not true. Because of all the preparation involved in commercials, the casting director generally runs a session for only a little while and then turns it over to a trusted employee who does the day's tapings or readings. The casting director's work is in choosing the people to be seen, working with the client, and negotiating with agents. However, usually before any tape is uploaded to cyberspace, the casting director reviews the work and listens to the people running the session, not only to hear about the actor's talent and skill, but often, more importantly, to assess the actor's attitude in the room that day. It doesn't help a freelance casting person to recommend an actor who will be difficult on the set or whose skills are not strong enough. For that reason, not all of the people put on tape are sent to be viewed by the producer/director, or by the ad agency in the case of a commercial.

In-house casting

There are also in-house casting directors who work for networks like NBC, or advertising agencies such as BBDO, or for companies such as Warner Brothers. They are usually salaried employees whose jobs often include hiring freelance casting people in various cities. These salaried casting people, either at networks or in ad agencies, are predominantly concerned with contracts and the business aspects of hiring actors and not so much with meeting the actors themselves. They too select a small number actors from the videos or readings to present to their employers. However, they usually only come into contact with the actors at the very end of the process when the actor "goes to network" or is finally presented to the advertising agency's client.

There are times when a network casting person will bypass a location casting director and go directly to the agents, but that is not a usual mode of doing business. In that case an agent may negotiate a taping fee. And, in these days of YouTube and instant upload videos, there are times when these casting folks will watch things submitted not only by agents, but also by actors themselves.

Real people casting

Real people casting is another form wherein casting directors seek not actors, but "real people." This is generally done for commercials. And, no, you are not a "real person" in the eyes of advertising agencies. I have cast both, and actors can never reproduce the fear of the camera and the wooden line deliveries that are the hallmark of real people. Real people casting, which often features lots of traveling, can involve finding and interviewing people who use certain products, who have certain hobbies or skills, or who work in a certain industry.

Real people casting is often called "street casting." My first foray into commercial casting was a "street" job. I had to find a class of 5-year-old children, a black surgeon, several tennis players, a Polish deli clerk, a canoer, and an elderly Chinese lady. It seemed to go on forever and in the days before cellphones I was completely dependent on my Polaroid camera, payphones, as well as a camera person to tote the great big video camera needed for interviews. I have stood on street corners and in public parks approaching college-age men who have tattoos all over their torsos, older men with certain types of beard, men and women who look like orchestra conductors, women who look like professional athletes, children who do bicycle tricks or who play ice hockey. Doing this sort of work takes charm and guts, it is tedious, exhausting, sometimes dangerous, and the weather is always bad for some reason.

In this day and age, people who become casting directors usually begin as interns or assistants in a casting office and work their way up. My former assistants, Rachel Tenner and Mickie Paskal, bought my casting business from me some years ago. Rachel subsequently sold her share to a former commercial casting person, Jennifer Rudnicke, and moved to LA where she began as an associate to Ellen Chenoweth before moving out on her own. She recently won an Emmy for her casting of the *Fargo* miniseries and works closely with Ben Stiller. I am sure that there is an intern or an associate in her office just waiting for the big chance.

One of the reasons that I give you all of this information is that you should understand that there are no insignificant people in casting offices. Casting directors use everyone in the office for information about the actors with whom they come into contact, either in the office or in their daily lives. These interns, assistants, or associates alert the casting directors about actors they may have seen in plays or those with whom they go to school. Erica Daniels, who was for years the casting director at the famed Steppenwolf Theatre, was an intern in my office while she was attending Northwestern University. Our office was hired to assist in the search for the bride in the remake of *Father of the Bride*. We contacted all of the agencies in the Midwest and called theatre departments near and far to find a beautiful and talented young woman of the right age. We saw many, many young ladies, some talented, some beautiful, some not so beautiful, and some who were not so young. Finally, Erica, who only worked a few days a week, asked if we had seen a classmate of hers, Kimberly Williams, now Kimberly Williams Paisley. This actress came in, taped and was cast almost immediately. I got the credit for this discovery, but I had nothing to do with it. As a matter of fact, I was at home with the flu when the taping took place. It was all Erica's doing.

Main title casting

In LA, casting people are experts not only in acting talent but also in the stars whose names enable the project to achieve its financing. They keep lists, scour the various rating systems, see every movie they possibly can, as well as keeping an eye on television and stage nationally. They spend a lot of time on the phone negotiating with the star's entourage of agents, managers, and lawyers. They may hire location casting directors if the shoot is out of LA, or travel to the location to cast themselves. Because of the very important job they do in getting a picture or series financed, they usually receive main title credit. Film directors generally hire the same casting director once they find one who understands their vision.

Many theatrical casting directors belong to a society called The Casting Society of America or CSA. It is the mark of a professional. To belong, a casting director must be sponsored by a member of CSA and have cast a significant project. This organization functions to promote the professionalism of its members, assistance with insurance and retirement, and as a means of awarding good work.

Extra casting

Extra casting is seldom done by theatrical casting directors. Extra casting directors are usually paid for the number of people they are assigned to supply and are often on the set functioning to corral the extras when needed. An extra in film is anyone who doesn't have a line and is not important to the story. They are called "atmosphere" or "background" players because their presence helps to establish where the story happens and what kinds of people live and work in that imaginary place. It is rare that an extra moves out of the crowd and into the film or series. There is a sort of caste system in Hollywood, the lowest being extras. The union does not oversee extras even though extra actors in LA have been campaigning for union protection. Working as an extra can pay as little as $50 a day and rarely more than $150 a day.

Commercial casting: extras

Extras in commercials are somewhat different. In a commercial, anyone who has anything to do with the product or the principal players in the spot, even if they have no lines, is a principal. Extras are those actors who are not linked to the product in any major way. So a flight attendant serving lunch to the spokeswoman for an airline would probably be a principal, but the person sitting next to the spokesperson reading a book would be an extra. Because extras in commercials are frequently "upgraded" on set, which means that they are given a line or some business having to do with the product or the principal performers, they become principals themselves. Because of how often this occurs, the SAG-AFTRA contract governing commercials has a rule requiring that the first twenty-six extras of any commercial be members of the union. The stigma against extras still exists to a degree, but in commercials it is disappearing. The pay for working as an extra in a commercial is quite good and many actors jump at the chance to do so.

Whether casting for film, TV, or legitimate stage, casting directors, unlike agents, are not associated with unions because they aren't responsible for paying actors, nor for collecting a commission from them. Their position with the unions requires them to follow union scale rules concerning how much an actor may be paid and how auditions need to be run. They are required to file union forms telling the union the names of actors who were at a session, when and for how long they were there, what their ages and ethnicities were, and how many auditions a particular actor has had for a specific project. Once an actor is cast, the casting director notifies and negotiates the actor's fee with the agent. They then alert the union of that occurrence and check to see that the actor is in good standing with the union or if they must join. Often they are asked to check the actor's citizenship status and other matters of that sort. In the case of film and TV, they are usually responsible for ensuring that the actor reports to the first day of the shoot on the right day and at the right time. If the actor is not a union member, the casting director must write an official letter of justification before that actor can be hired and passed on by the union. There is a lot of paperwork involved!

Regardless of the type of CD, the job of finding people and presenting them to production teams remains the same. For most of us the best part of the job is helping actors to work and in being a part of the project's success. The worst part is that there is never enough time. Even in this day of cyber communications, the job demands enormous energy and stamina.

Personal talent managers and agents

Personal managers are people who actually manage an actor's career. The unions do not license them, nor can they legally negotiate contracts for the actor. In Los Angeles and New York, they must be allied to SAG-AFTRA-AEA agents in order to practice their profession. Currently personal managers operate in LA and NYC, and they are beginning to appear in Chicago. While they cannot negotiate contracts directly, they usually work with an actor's agent to make sure that the performer is making the maximum amount of money available and getting proper billing.

Their function is to be the actor's advocate to the business, to do the phone calls and the research that actors cannot do for themselves. They can submit actors for projects, make sure that casting directors are aware of the actors they represent, obtain representation for actors without agents, and acquaint producers and directors with the actor's work. Unlike many agents, they are committed to a small group of actors whose careers they attempt to shape.

Agents generally have many more clients and are dependent on a volume business to make their livings. Managers charge between 10 and 20 percent of an actor's performing income regardless of how that income was obtained. The contract between the actor and the manager is fashioned by the management company. Some management contracts are for three years, some for one year, and some for five years. In working with an agent as opposed to a manager, an actor may sever ties with the agent whenever he or she has been without work for ninety days, or the agent may drop an actor after the same amount of time if they desire to do so. A management contract may not be so easy to get out of and for that reason it is very important for performers to enter into management contracts with a good deal of legal advice.

Personal managers are essentially counselors for their clients and star salespeople for the business. Good ones have many contacts and an understanding of how to position a particular actor's career for maximum success. Legitimate managers never charge money until their clients are employed. Having a manager can be very expensive because you will have to pay your agent the standard 10 percent as well as paying your manager an additional 10–20 percent. This can reduce your paycheck by as much as 30 percent.

"Plus ten" is never applicable to your contract with a manager. You will need to pay the manager a percentage on the entire amount.

It is possible that your agreement with your manager means that your employment check will go directly to them. The manager will then deduct the percentage you owe and issue you a check directly. The ways of payment in the business are many and varied; your agent may pay you through your manager, or your check may go directly to your checking account through a payment agency, depending on contractual agreements.

For young actors, a manager can be a real asset if the manager is well established with access to casting directors and agents. They can open doors that may be closed. However, if a manager is interested in an actor who has no real credits beyond schooling, he or she should be closely examined for legitimacy. It may be that because of the expertise of a manager, he or she will commit to an inexperienced actor—it has been known to happen successfully.

My manager saw me in a short that was in a film festival in Brooklyn and saw something in me that he apparently wanted to work with. I'm not sure what it was exactly but he reached out to me while I was still a student, which built a lot of trust (which is everything in an actor/manager relationship) because he was willing to take a chance on me and believed in me before anything had even begun. He guides me through the chaos of the business that I wouldn't even know how to approach.

ALEX KOCH, Actor, *Under the Dome*

If you are familiar with Alex, you will know he is a wonderful young actor, very skillful and possessive of real depth. He is also very handsome and that makes him an attractive package for an agent or a manager. I am not diminishing Alex's talent in any way, he is simply lucky enough to have been born under the right stars. Another LA actor—you would know him if you saw him, but he wishes to be anonymous—had the following to say: "I have had managers and I have no idea what managers do."

Many legitimate personal managers belong to the National Conference of Personal Managers, Inc. (NCOPM) or the Talent Managers Association (TMA), both of which have a code of ethics for their members. Their websites are easily available: **www. Talentmanagers.org** and **www.NCOPM.com**.

The relationships that actors develop with casting directors, agents, and managers are the most important and long lasting of their professional life. Directors come and directors go, producers come and producers go, but the casting directors, the agents, and managers are a constant presence and must be cultivated and honored as significant aids to an actor's career.

8

Building a Character: Type Versus Brand

How will you be perceived in your Life Play? How will you present yourself? While nobody wants to be typecast, it's going to happen one way or another. Your age, your dialect, your training, your ethnicity, your height, your teeth, and your attitudes towards life will all be a part of this typing. Each one of us is unique and it is that uniqueness that creates your brand. A brand includes many facets and is not a "type." Think of the Coca-Cola company, it has Diet Coke, Sprite, Mr. Pibb, Classic Coke, Cherry Coke, and others.

Once Coke was established as a quality company, it went on to capitalize on its good reputation and branched out into other sorts of soft drinks. It did not decide that because people liked Coca-Cola the company should begin making computers. Coke knew its market and expanded by moving past simple Coke to other flavors. Actors need to do the same thing. Begin to think of your best flavor and then expand on it to include a full range of products. I am not suggesting that you "type" yourself. Your job is to present yourself in such a way that someone who has never met you will be able to imagine casting you.

Ask yourself why directors and agents and casting people typecast? We do it all the time; our brains are wired to think in categories. Consider the times when you have played casting director with your friends. You sit around and try to envision how you might cast an upcoming movie, or novel, or play. Some of you may decide that looks are the most important element in casting, and others may believe that it is the personal human qualities of an actor that makes for good casting. Directors and casting directors do the same thing. Like you, they don't cast actors who they wish to stretch; they cast *people*. Some are sure that looks are the most important element and some prefer a more subtle approach to casting. Why would anyone decide to cast a person who they felt was wrong for a role?

Like Coca-Cola, you can control this to a degree. The first part of this is accepting what the world is telling you before you can move forward. As an actor, you want to be and do everything. However, as with basketball, we can't all slam dunk the ball. There are certain physical requirements to do so. There is a saying in Alcoholics Anonymous, "Acceptance is the key to all of our problems." I think that this is probably right. It doesn't, however, imply that you should therefore accept that you are too ugly, fat, old, untrained, or whatever, and therefore unable to perform in whatever arena in which you are interested.

Once you accept your supposed limitations, see them as unique qualities to be exploited and adjusted to your advantage. Speaking of slam dunks, I once saw a basketball player whose name was Spud Webb, who was 5'7". He had two things going for him—speed that enabled him to whiz around the court before the big guys even saw him, and an amazing ability to jump over four feet high. As a very young player, he concentrated on developing those skills. It took him much longer than the tall players to receive recognition and he was always fighting to overcome the belief that height was required to play. Even when he was chosen from among 5,000 athletes to play on the Texas High School All State team, no major college recruited him. He went to a junior college where he once again had to prove his skills. After two years there, he was finally chosen by North Carolina State University and went on to be a leading player in the Sweet 16. Even after that, no NBA team picked him up. He played instead for the US Basketball League for the next two years, and at last, in 1985, the Detroit Pistons drafted him in the fourth round. It would seem that his dream had come true, but he was cut very soon afterwards. A lesser man would have packed it in and gone home. But Spud finally found a home with the Atlanta Hawks in 1985 where he went on to a much lauded career, and in 1986 he won the slam-dunk championship, beating players like Michael Jordan and Dominique Wilkins. Spud developed his own game and, in the end, became the basketball player that he had dreamed of becoming. He overcame his "type" through concentration on his unique talents, a disregard for his supposed deficiencies, an enormous amount of practice, and lots of patience.

Spud's life can't be seen as simply "Well, he really wanted it!" It reveals how a dream is activated, and shows how hard life can be when you don't fit anyone's idea of "type." It took a great deal for Spud to convince any of the coaches to even grant him a tryout; they were blinded by their own prejudices.

Most actors that I know would have been devastated by the kinds of obstacles that Spud faced; not everyone has his kind of grit. You need to take a good long look at yourself to discover if you have the moxie to buck the odds like Spud, or whether you would prefer to play in a game more suited to your willpower and your dreams. Not everyone needs to be a star like Spud did. There are many, many actors who are very happy making a living doing commercials and voiceovers, staying in smaller cities, and many choose to do artistically valuable local theatre, or teach high school theatre. Those choices are as honorable and admirable as the decision to move to New York for a chance at Broadway.

Really good directors and casting directors understand what the rejecting basketball coaches didn't; a player is more than a body. A player, no matter how well suited to the game, needs heart, patience, and determination. Talent is irrelevant if the player is lazy or lacking in the drive to succeed.

In show business, the best directors don't cast exactly "to type." They are aware that there needs to be some distance between the actor and the character. It's not that there is some great virtue in "not playing oneself," it is that dissonance is always mysterious. I once had dinner with Jessica Chastain, who was a friend of one of my students. She was not very well known at the time and I had no idea who she was; she seemed like an ordinary acting student. As we sat at the table, I saw a very delicate young woman with fair skin and red hair, who, as the evening went on, revealed herself to be a shy, curious, sensitive, generous, and funny woman with a talent for enjoying life. In a recent article, she said that when she began her career, her red hair and pale looks were a detriment and shut her out of getting auditions. Many actors would have then dyed their hair and gone to tanning parlors in an attempt to fit into the latest fashionable look. Luckily, Jessica decided to be true to herself and use what she had rather than emulating something someone else had.

Her Academy Award-nominated performance as a CIA intelligence analyst in *Zero Dark Thirty* was nothing like the girl with whom I had dinner, but her intelligence seemed to lead the way in the role while her physical delicacy provided some distance.

Most of you might think that she had all the breaks, that she was beautiful or that somehow she had gotten lucky, or that she had money. However, few people will take the time to see the middle-class girl who realized that she wanted to act when she was seven, became a passionate actress while in high school, went on to a state college for a few years, and did lots and lots of plays in her area. She entered Julliard at the age of 22 where she graduated when she was 26. After graduation, she worked both on stage and in films (many of which were badly reviewed) before her career really began to blossom when she was cast in *The Help* at the age of 34. That was eight years following graduation.

In an interview with *Vanity Fair* she said, "I've spent my life being embarrassed." This may account for her having ". . . played a lot of girls who had something off. Maybe they'd been the victim of some horrible accident. Or they were crazy." Again, it was probably her very sensitive nature that did it. However, if you look at Ms Chastain, it is obvious that she is an actress whose uniqueness took some time to be recognized and when it was, she soared to heights she may never have expected.

There are many other stories like this one about how actors overcame prejudices because of their beauty or lack thereof. The major lesson is that we are each unique because we are all human, and we need to seek people and places where that uniqueness can be a plus. Once you accept that because of your singularity there are a certain number of roles for which you are exactly right, a certain number of them where you will have to stretch, and a certain number that you will probably never get to play, you can begin. It may take you longer if you don't fit anyone's definition of a type, and you may have to wait till someone finally "gets you," but most success involves simply sticking around, working hard, and being ready. This is your Life Play, not anyone else's. Rondi Reed, a Tony Award-winning actress, for her work in *August: Osage County* on Broadway, and currently featured on CBS sitcom *Mike and Molly*, wrote the following:

> In high school and later college I was "a character actress" which is what happens to those of us who are not tall, thin, and blonde. I became ruthlessly aware of my obvious strengths—big energy, strong vocal, and physical presence, and toughness. I played them all up whenever I could. I was labeled intense and a bit too much at times, but everyone knew that I was very hard working. I was not a high school star, nor a college standout. I did happen to hang out with a like-minded group of theatre geeks in college who later founded Steppenwolf Theatre in Chicago, who asked me to join them in 1980 when they needed a character actress. Lucky girl: me.
>
> It was much later in my career when auditioning for a production of Shaw's Arms and the Man *that the director Sheldon Patinkin told me he believed that I was an ingenue in a character actress body. He cast me as Louka, the young servant girl who gets hot and bothered around a pompous soldier who has come to woo the other girl in the show, the "other" ingenue.*
>
> I was flabbergasted and terrified and it changed my life. All sorts of doors began to swing open, not only in my acting career, but also in my mind. Sheldon's gift gave me the power to allow my inner self to emerge, and I realized that self could reside in ALL my characters regardless of type or age. I refused to pigeonhole myself anymore and in my forties and even early fifties played leading ladies and romantic leads and no one questioned if I belonged there. My difference was now seen as my strength, and my newfound vulnerability made me beautiful in my own way.
>
> Granted, I would most likely never play Juliet or Emily in Our Town, *but owing to my new view of myself, I was not relegated to every mother, hooker, and next-door neighbor in the play. I do know there are roles that I have been completely right for, Martha in* Who's Afraid of Virginia Woolf?, *the Nurse in* Romeo and Juliet, *Big Mama in* Cat on A Hot Tin Roof, *my beloved Madame Morrible in* Wicked *and Mattie Fae, the role Tracy Letts wrote for me in* August: Osage County. *I have been lucky to play them in wonderful situations with terrific casts and consider myself*

blessed. I have also worked hard, fallen down and got up more times than I can count, and was ready to walk away, BUT I did not. And that has made all the difference!

Adjusting to yourself

Again, the Myers-Briggs can help. If you have answered honestly, the Myers-Briggs personality profile can help you in discovering your own brand. It has done most of the work for you. It doesn't say anything about how you look (that's good). It <u>does</u> say a lot about how you might feel, how you project yourself into the world, and how you might work best in it. You don't have to trust me, ask a friend if your Myers-Briggs seems right. Nine times out of ten they will agree.

For instance, if your profile says that you are an ISFP, here is the explanation of those qualities and some suggestions of how to incorporate them in your brand. This is from the webpage **http://www.personalitypage.com**.

ISFPs generally have the following traits:

- Keen awareness of their environment.
- Live in the present moment.
- Enjoy a slower pace—they like to take time to savor the present moment.
- Dislike dealing with theory or abstract thought, unless they see a practical application.
- Faithful and loyal to people and ideas which are important to them.
- Individualistic, having no desire to lead or follow.
- Take things seriously, although they frequently appear not to do so.
- Special bond with children and animals.
- Quiet and reserved, except with people they know extremely well.

- Trusting, sensitive, and kind.

- Service-oriented; they're driven to help others.

- Extremely well-developed appreciation for aesthetic beauty.

- Likely to be original and unconventional.

- Learn best with hands-on training.

- Hate being confined to strict schedules and regimens.

- Need space and freedom to do things their own way.

- Dislike mundane, routine tasks, but will perform them if necessary.

The ISFP is a very special individual who needs to have a career that is more than a job. The middle of the road is not likely to be a place where they will be fulfilled and happy. They need to have a career that is consistent with their strong core of inner values. Since they *prefer to live in the current moment, and take the time to savor it*, they do not do well in some of the more fast-paced corporate environments. They need a *great deal of space and freedom* if they are going to function in their natural realm of *acute sensory awareness*. If they give free reign to their natural abilities, they may find a wonderful artist within themselves. Almost every major artist in the world has been an ISFP. Since the ISFP is so *acutely aware of people's feelings and reactions*, and is driven by their inner values to help people, the ISFP *is also a natural counselor and teacher*.

The following list of professions is built on our impressions of careers which would be especially suitable for an ISFP. It is meant to be a starting place, rather than an exhaustive list. There are no guarantees that any or all of the careers listed here would be appropriate for you, or that your best career match is among those listed.

Possible career paths for the ISFP

- Artist.

- Musician/composer.

- Designer.

- Child care/early childhood development.

- Social worker/counselor.

- Teacher.

- Psychologist.

- Veterinarian.

- Forest ranger.

When you look at your "type," you can see that your own leanings can be the beginning of your brand. You are very likely to be cast based on those aspects of your personality if you draw attention to them. If you are an ISFP, as in the example given, having one of your pictures taken in a wardrobe that suggests you spend time in nature (not a forest ranger's outfit please) might help a commercial casting person get an idea of how to use you. Be aware though, pictures should *suggest*, not *limit*, casting. So it would be inappropriate to go the full nine yards and dress yourself as Paul Bunyan.

Also, if you happen to be an ISFP, in order to reveal your sensitive nature, perhaps a shot with very little make-up, soft hair, and a subtly toned sweater or a loose-fitting and casual linen shirt might convey this quality. Such a shot could make you a great choice for a young person in love—useful for romantic roles, or sweet young mothers, or men with a warm and fuzzy side. If you don't have that quality, don't emphasize it; if you do, play into it.

The ISFP list also includes the "artist." You probably have some idea about how artists look and dress, something quirky in the fabric, perhaps some scarves or vests or great ties. Generally a picture showing an artistic side should be relaxed and minimal unless the ISFP wants to emphasize intensity. How many actors do this wearing a black turtleneck? I am not suggesting one (they are an awful cliché these days), but they can still work. A picture that represents your artistic side would be very useful for films and stage.

Your agent will need more than one picture of you, but he or she will choose the ones that they believe shows your strong suit as well as your most castable look. If you have more than one agent, as is often the case in New York and LA, your commercial agent will want one look and your "legit" agent (theatre and film) will want another.

You will also want a variety of them to take to auditions or to send out when seeking employment.

When you establish a brand, you are giving people a menu of the various ways they can use you without using their imaginations. You are casting yourself. Don't expect casting people to work hard to see how to use you: show them. In order to do so, you must also realize that at the beginning of your career you will be doing lots of auditioning—at first, monologues, then presentation scenes or cold readings, depending on where you are working. You will have little control over what you are asked to read for, but you do have control over what monologues or presentation scenes you choose to do. I will address this in the chapter devoted to auditioning, but suffice it to say that whatever your choices are, they should reflect your picture and your résumé to make one understandable statement about you in the world.

Oddly enough, once you have established a brand within your market, and you have accepted yourself as having something of value to give, you will be asked to audition for things not at all obvious from the menu you presented at first. I think this is because, when you appear to know who you are and how you are best used, you give off an inviting air of confidence.

9

Doing Your Life Play:
Action!

Once you are finally represented by an agent, it is not time to relax. Many young actors get an agent and then expect that they can go about their merry way while the agent takes over. I wish that this were possible, but the agent's job is to send you on auditions and to make sure you are paid properly. Until you become a major moneymaker for any particular agency, they will often pay little attention to you except to make sure you don't make enemies of the casting directors, and that you show up at the right time and place. Some agents will respond if you have a specific question or need, some may not. You are in charge of everything else. Let's look at the five things you must do to make sure you are on everyone's list.

1 Maintain a database of all your industry contacts

Show business is unlike many others in that it is always quasi-personal. If you keep a database, you will be able to work more personally with the people for whom you audition. Another plus in keeping a database is that you will be able to formulate strategies once you recognize patterns such as, "Jane Peterson, the casting director, has only called me in for cop roles," or "John Ramirez, the casting director, hasn't called me in since February of last year," or "Sean Ainsley, commercial director with Commercials R Us, always calls me back and I have worked for his company several times." All of these observations can lead to more action on your part. If Jane Peterson only sees you as a cop but you feel that you are castable in other roles, you can begin a campaign of new pictures and invitations to shows, and request your agent to push a bit harder and lift you out of the "cop" niche. If John Ramirez hasn't called you in since February, you might want to write a personal letter to him expressing your desire to be seen by his agency or ask your agent to call John to determine what you need to do to be back on his list of people to see. And if Sean Ainsley is a fan, you might want to send him invitations to shows, or a Birthday or Christmas card.

Your database may be kept online, in a box, or in a notebook, whatever is easiest for you. I encourage you to do this on your computer and to have a back-up as well. The database should contain the following:

- The name, organization, address, phone and email of the directors, casting directors, casting assistants, interns, and any other industry people you've met.

- The date or dates of your contact, and what the circumstances were. Include what you wore, anything special that was said, and other such information.

- If your contact with that person was an audition, keep a list of callbacks and castings. After a while it can be helpful to determine your "batting average." In Los Angeles, it wouldn't be odd for an actor to book one job for every twelve auditions.

2 Maintain ongoing communication with industry contacts

Once your database is up and running, you should plan a monthly mailing of postcards with your name, agent, and picture on one side and a brief note on the other. If you aren't in a show, let the industry person know that you are taking a great class, or in other ways actively pursuing excellence in your career.

3 Take classes and coaching

Regularly take audition classes for both on-camera work and stage work. If you get a script that you think you can nail, get coaching from someone who understands the media for which the script is written. If you can't afford a professional coach, ask an actor who works a lot to give you some pointers. Most people like to be helpful; it makes them feel good.

A well-rounded actor should have the knowledge not only of how to audition/act on camera and on the stage, but methods currently being used by practitioners throughout the world. In order to do this, you will want to study long term with teachers whose main focus is on the art of acting rather than the semi-technical demands of such things as appearing on camera, voiceover techniques, monologue, or song preparation, or other more mundane areas of preparation.

In almost every city there are teachers of substance who are not in the "business" at all. Here are some things you should consider before taking a class with a local teacher. As you watch a class, be aware that it is almost impossible for any teacher to have a complete class of amazing people. In general, classes have mixed levels of talent and training. Do not be discouraged unless the teacher praises poor work in order to make the actor feel good. A professional teacher should be able to give potentially difficult criticism without destroying an actor, and without giving untruthful feedback.

Also, check to see if the teacher has a method or a vocabulary from which to work, or if he or she is simply directing. There are many people who can direct an actor into a good performance, but such coaching may not be helpful to the actor whose final aim must be to work in rehearsals without needing a good director. As you watch, ask yourself if the teacher's comments seem to assist the actors or simply impress them. Unfortunately, there are many people who profess to be acting specialists, but who simply want to be gurus.

Does the teacher work with a scene or not? There are some who don't work on a scene but do give great advice that is to be followed up in a later class, and there are those who work on a part of a scene in class. There are good reasons for both types of teachers and you may personally prefer one or the other. A teacher who doesn't work a scene but gives pointers to the actors may actually be doing them a favor because he or she is forcing the performers to take care of themselves. A teacher who works scenes or parts of scenes in class is often better for actors whose technique is not as developed as it could be.

If the teacher seems to be talking more than watching scenes, if they share lots of stories about their lives as performers or about celebrities they have known, they may be less than helpful. The best teachers talk very little, say only what needs to be said, and ask lots of questions. Look for this in your potential instructors.

You might also want to find out the teacher's philosophy of acting. There are many schools of acting pedagogy but the best of them begin with a base in Stanislavski's concept, called the *theory of physical action*. If you have not studied a lot of acting, you may believe that the Stanislavski work means "The Method" and you may have heard that the "Method" was not a very good way of working. "The Method" was created by Lee Strasberg, and in the final analysis has very little to do with Stanislavski. Stanislavski referred to his work as "The System".

Historically, the most influential theoreticians whose work was solidly based in Stanislavski include Uta Hagen, Stella Adler, Sanford Meisner, Michael Shurtleff, Bobby Lewis, Harold Clurman, and others. Each of these now deceased teachers inspired many thousands of performers and teachers and each had a different means of approaching truthfulness for actors. A good teacher should be familiar with all of them and be able to tell you which of them have guided their own thought. Most of them wrote or were written about and you can do some reading on your own before deciding what sort of work appeals to you. Be careful of teachers who simply say that they do their own thing. The wheel has been invented, the craft is obtainable, and if a teacher wants to remain mysterious it may be wise of you to find one who can communicate more clearly.

There are excellent newer approaches that, consciously or not, incorporate Stanislavski. One of these is a system called "Viewpoints," formulated by the director and scholar, Ann Bogart. She devised her method based partially on a combination of work with her mentor Tadashi Suzuki, and on an earlier "Viewpoints" method created by modern dance pioneers, Mary Overlie and Wendell Beavers. "Viewpoints" is based in physical training and is a very flexible way of encountering a scene or a play, useful to actors and to directors as well. Most of these more physically-based teachers also owe a debt to the pioneering work created by Jerzy Grotowski at the Theatre Laboratory in Poland. Many directors have been trained in this method and knowing this language can be very advantageous.

Viola Spolin, a social worker and theatre person who developed a way of helping children using theatre games in the early days of the settlement house movement in Chicago created an entire philosophy of theatre-making using improvisation. Her impact on the theatre, both improvisational and scripted, remains as revolutionary as Stanislavski's system. Stanislavski had used improvisations extensively, but never actually discussed how to create them, nor how to use them outside of the text. Spolin wrote several books sharing her techniques, and her *Improvisation for the Theatre* is in the library of most good acting teachers because improvisation is one of the most powerful tools for rehearsals that an actor can master. Spolin's approach and her *Theater Games* gave birth to the entire improvisational theatre movement. Her son, Paul Sills, founded the famous Second City which in turn spawned improvisational companies across the world. In England, Spolin's writing inspired another revolutionary teacher of improvisation, Keith Johnstone, whose books *Impro* and *Improvisation for Storytellers* are classics.

Two warnings

- There are teachers who don't allow observers because they feel it will interfere with the work. However, if you cannot observe a class, you will have no way of knowing whether the teacher is appropriate for you or not. If you have to pay to take the class sight unseen, be careful. I also suspect that if the class is so very private and precious that an occasional visitor unduly disrupts the students in it, such actors will be unable to withstand the workaday world of acting.

- Don't be a "smorgasbord" kind of student. A little knowledge is a dangerous thing! In order to know anything, it is best to know it deeply. Too many actors and some teachers think that sampling classes is a good way to learn. In my opinion, it only leads to performers who understand a little bit about a lot of things, but nothing real about anything.

4 Be in shows

It should be obvious that actors need to act. If you are not in a class, you should be in a show. As I have stated earlier, the shows you choose to be in, and the companies producing them, should be of quality and in a decent location. It is your job to know who the best companies and directors are, and to see as much of the work in your town as you can. (The number of aspiring actors who come to study privately with me who never actually see actors working on stage flabbergasts me.)

If you are not cast at good theatres with strong actors, stay in class until you become ready to be cast at that level. I am not saying that you need to be on Broadway, or at the Mark Taper or at the Goodman or at the Alley Theatre. There are many small companies, all over the country, doing wonderful work. These smaller companies (we call them "storefronts" in Chicago) are the richest places for actors to test their wings. Often the shows that these companies can afford to produce are more exciting than those done by their big brothers. There are many amazing directors, actors, and designers working in the off-off-off theatre movement whose work rivals anything that you can see anywhere. The people doing the small shows are the people who in five years will be doing the big ones.

So do your homework—the last thing you want to do is to be in a bad show with a group of energetic dilettantes or with directors who are less qualified than you are to direct. Such experiences can harm your ego, your pocketbook, and possibly your reputation.

Many actors these days are gaining access through creating solo performances. If you find some subject matter that interests you, this sort of endeavor can keep you artistically alive when the world around you seems dreary. Solo performances are gaining in popularity, and they are usually short and inexpensive to produce. They can be booked for off nights at theatres, especially if the tech demands are very light. If you have never seen such a show, Google the works of John Leguizamo, Spaulding Gray, or Lily Tomlin. There are several books concerning how to do this work and I will include some of them in the final chapter of this book.

With easy access to cameras and the internet, more and more actors are videotaping and submitting themselves directly without the aid of agents for both film/TV and stage. Do not be afraid to do this, and if it is a bad tape, and you hate it, don't send it! Actor's Access (**www.actorsaccess.com**) and the Casting Network (**www. castingnetworks.com**) frequently release such casting calls.

10

Your Life Play:
Résumés

A résumé is a one-page document that allows the industry to know who you are, who you know, what you do, and who has stamped your book. It is very much a part of "Who you know." It complements your picture in that the info on the résumé should seem somehow to match the picture of the person attached to it.

When you are first starting out, don't be ashamed that you have no major motion picture credits, nor big Broadway starring roles to list. Casting directors and agents understand that you are beginning and that you will be amassing credits as your career moves ahead. List your school and community credits proudly; there is no need to pad a résumé or to be dishonest.

A theatrical résumé is not in any way like a business résumé. You may be tempted to consult a "career" adviser at school or in the corporate world to create your résumé. However, they will not be familiar with the unique format required of an acting résumé which is simply a series of lists, single-spaced, including:

1 Credits: shows/films you have done, who directed them, where and for whom they were done.

2 Education and the names of your teachers.

3 Skills you possess that might contribute to the project being cast.

4 Union affiliations i.e. SAG, AEA, AEA eligible, SAG eligible, etc.

The document must be headed with your name, enlarged and in bold type. If possible a thumbnail of you featuring a photo different than the one attached to your résumé should be in the upper left hand corner. Your name is generally centered at the top of the document. Do not be too creative with fonts; simply be clear. Too many design elements in your résumé will make it seem as if you are not aware of "how things are done." Under your name include your union status if you have any. If not leave it blank.

WALTER BRODY

SAG, AFTRA, AEA, AGVA

Under your name or union affiliations, if you have any, you need to include a way to reach you. When you are first beginning you will need to use your cellphone number. Some actors also put their email or website URL under their contact number.

Once you have an agent, you will remove your cell number and use the agency contact under your name. Often an agency will give you their logo to print directly on your résumé. In that case it should be in the upper right-hand corner on the same level as your name. The structure of these identifiers is somewhat flexible, but the general template is as I have described it.

WALTER BRODY

SAG, AFTRA, AEA
Jbrody@blogspot.com

Stewart Talent
(312) 943 3131

Off to one side or the other, it is generally accepted practice to include your height, weight, hair color, and color of eyes. Do not include an age range on a professional résumé; it can only limit you. The only time you will be asked about your age is if you are auditioning for a liquor commercial in which case you must be at least 25. That, however, is only between you and your agent, not for public consumption. In most markets, actors don't include clothing sizes or any of that sort of information in their acting résumé.

JANE DRAKE BRODY

5'1", 124 lbs.   SAG, AFTRA, AEA
Gray hair   jbrody@blogspot.com   Stewart Talent
Brown eyes   312 943-3131

If you are a singer and this résumé is focused towards that work, your general range, alto, soprano, baritone, or whatever, should be included in the upper right-hand corner. If you want to indicate your actual range, it is generally written Bb–3C or indicated on a musical staff.

JANE DRAKE BRODY

5'1", 124 lbs.   SAG, AFTRA, AEA
Gray hair   jbrody@blogspot.com
Brown eyes   Stewart Talent
          312 943-3131
          Contralto
          Bb–3C

Your credits

Credits *should not be* listed chronologically, but by importance of role, director, or theatre. In deciding how to do this, you should also understand that well-known plays are more important to list at the top, rather than plays that no one knows. The reason for this is that most people reading your résumé will read the first three or so credits, then scan the rest to see if they are familiar with any of the theatres or directors with whom you have worked.

Commercial credits are not listed in major markets. In order to indicate that you have done commercials, it is usual to insert the following phrase, "Commercial list available upon request." As an actress, I used this phrase on my résumé and diligently kept my list in case anyone asked. No one ever did, so don't sweat it. If you haven't done any commercials, don't utilize the phrase on your résumé; you will simply be lying, which is not allowed!

For your stage and film credits, it is accepted practice to use three or four columns. The first is the name of the show, the second the role you played, the third, the director, and the fourth the name of the theatre where you appeared or the studio network producing the project. If you appeared with a star, his or her name should be included in some fashion. Each geographical area of the country has a different way of separating your credits, and each medium will also expect different things.

In New York, for stage, you should generally separate New York credits from regional credits, and sometimes Broadway is separated from "off Broadway," or "musical theatre" may be separated from "straight plays." Keep in mind that your résumé is there to help you put your best foot forward. It is not a legal document. I don't mean that you should ever lie on your résumé, but you can highlight your credits using various categories.

Example: New York

JANE DRAKE BRODY   Stewart Talent

5'1", 124 lbs	SAG, AFTRA, AEA		312 943-3131
Gray hair	jbrody@blogspot.com		Contralto
Brown eyes			Bb–3C

B'dway

The Tree of Life	Ella	dir. Jerry Long	Neil Simon Theatre
Make My Day	Lillian	dir. Max Martin	Shubert Theatre

B'dway Tour

Life of Martha	Martha	with Mary London (big star lady)	Joe Shmoe prod.

Regional

Romeo and Juliet	Nurse	dir. Wendy Drake	Indiana Repertory
Macbeth	Lady Macbeth	"	"

Film

Having our Say	Jane	dir. Bob Cohen	Warner Brothers
The Woman Who	Chloe	dir. Larson Bole	True Light Prod.

TV

Fun with Pets	Betty (guest star)		ABC
The Candle	Dolores		CBS

TRAINING

MFA, Acting, Big School University
LeCoq Training, Jean Val Jean, Paris
Viewpoints and Suzuki, Citi Company, NYC

Special Skills: Proficient in acrobatics and circus skills of all types, Russian speaker, ballet (12 yrs), Tap (10 yrs), Jazz Dance (10 yrs) SAFD certified, excellent at dialects.

Example: Los Angeles

In Los Angeles, your SAG film credits, if you had a speaking role, must be first. Many film résumés don't include any stage work at all, but that is a question that will be decided by your particular agency. Again, commercials are never listed nor included.

JANE DRAKE BRODY   Stewart Talent

5'1", 124 lbs   SAG, AFTRA, AEA   312 943-3131
Gray hair   jbrody@blogspot.com   Contralto
Brown eyes   Bb–3C

Film

Having our Say	Jane	dir., Bob Cohen	Warner Brothers
The Woman Who	Chloe	dir. Larson Bole	True Light Prod.

TV

Fun with Pets	Betty (guest star)		ABC
The Candle	Dolores		CBS

B'dway

The Tree of Life	Ella	dir. Jerry Long	Neil Simon Theatre
Make My Day	Lillian	dir. Max Martin	Shubert Theatre

B'dway Tour

Life of Martha	Martha (with big star)	dir. Mary London	Joe Shmoe prod.

Regional

Romeo and Juliet	Nurse	dir. Wendy Drake	Indiana Repertory
Macbeth	Lady Macbeth	"	"

Training: MFA, Acting, Big School University

On-camera techniques, Bob Watterson, Bob Watterson Studio, Los Angeles

LeCoq training, Jean Val Jean, Paris, France

Viewpoints and Suzuki- Citi Company, NYC

SPECIAL SKILLS: professional level horseback riding, drive stick shift and can handle farm equipment, high level of skill at both ice skating and roller skating, dog show handler, skilled at softball, baseball, soccer, and gymnastics of every kind, proficient in acrobatics and circus skills of all types, Russian speaker, ballet (12 yrs), tap (10 yrs), jazz dance (10 yrs).

SAFD certified, excellent at dialects.

Example: theatre

On a résumé for theatre, AEA theatres should be listed first, films second. If the résumé is for film and TV, the categories are reversed.

JANE DRAKE BRODY

Stewart Talent
312 943-3131
Contralto
Bb–3C

5'1", 124 lbs
Gray hair
Brown eyes

SAG, AFTRA, AEA
jbrody@blogspot.com

Stage

The Tree of Life	Ella	dir. Jerry Long	Neil Simon Theatre
Make My Day	Lillian	dir. Max Martin	Shubert Theatre
Life of Martha (big star name)	Martha	dir. Mary London	Joe Shmoe Prod.
Romeo and Juliet	Nurse	dir. Wendy Drake	Indiana Repertory
Macbeth	Lady Macbeth	"	"

Film

Having our Say	Jane	dir. Bob Cohen	Warner Brothers
The Woman Who	Chloe	dir. Larson Bole	True Light Prod.

TV

Fun with Pets	Betty (guest star)		ABC
The Candle	Dolores		CBS

TRAINING:

MFA, Acting, Big School University

On-camera Techniques, Bob Watterson
LeCoq training, Jean Val Jean, Paris
Viewpoints and Suzuki-Citi Company, NYC

SPECIAL SKILLS: professional level horseback riding, drive stick shift, can handle farm equipment, high level of skill at both ice skating and roller skating, dog show handler, skilled at softball, baseball, soccer, and gymnastics of every kind, proficient in acrobatics and circus skills of all types, Russian speaker, ballet (12 yrs), tap (10 yrs), jazz dance (10 yrs). SAFD certified, excellent at dialects.

Other factors in choosing how to structure your credit lists

Doing a very small role on Broadway is better than doing *Hamlet* at the Alaska Repertory unless you are in Alaska in which case that credit may be topmost. When you have amassed a lot of credits, the heading for theatre or film, depending on which you lead with, will be "representative credits." You will edit the credits that are not advantageous to you.

Teachers of note

You should make a study of your teachers to determine whether they are well-known or not. While in school, you may simply know them as George or Barbara. However, in the professional world they may be well-known not only as teachers but also as performers, casting directors, directors, agents, or singers. Most theatre people teach at some point in their lives, and that doesn't negate their standing within show biz.

Don't list commercials

Why shouldn't you list commercials? The reason for this is not only artistic, but also because there is a rule in commercial-land that says if a performer has a commercial running or on hold, he or she may not legally do a commercial for a competing product. For instance, if you have a commercial running for Joe's Hamburgers, you would be forbidden to do a commercial for Bob's Great Big Hamburger Stand. This is logical, right? However, many advertising agencies are leery of using you if you have *ever* done a commercial for a fast food chain regardless of when it was done, or where, or for how long it played. This is plainly not in the rulebook, but it has been known to occur.

Special skills to include

The special skills section is more important for film and TV than it is for stage. Your stage skills such as stage combat are important to theatre people. However, movies, series, and commercials frequently feature people doing mundane activities such as playing soccer or building a brick wall. It is helpful to list such skills as long as you are decently skilled at them.

Additionally, special skills can give the auditor a better picture of who you are. For instance, if you played minor league baseball before becoming an actor, that will be of interest. Or if you are a published novelist, it assists the casting people in seeing more about you. At least it is something to talk about in an interview or audition other than your last show.

As a former casting director, it was always refreshing to meet an actor who had interests other than performing. When I was casting a made-for-TV movie quite a few years ago, an actor had included in his skills section that he played horse polo. As it happened, the director of the project also played horse polo. The actor was hired for the run of the picture, partially so that the two of them could play polo on location. Another actor shared that he was a computer specialist whose hobby was building computers. He was so fascinating when he talked about it that he was cast in a decent sized role that demanded a brainy guy. I am not saying that either of these actors was untalented or unfit for the roles they were offered, however, in these instances, the little bit of further information was all it took to interest the director in hiring them.

Dialects

It is perhaps smarter to say "very proficient with dialects" or "great ear for dialects" rather than listing them. In this way, if you haven't listed the dialect a casting person wants, you won't be rejected out of hand. If, however, you want to list your dialects, be very careful that you are really, really good. If you have listed a dialect that you learned long ago, or that you never quite mastered, it is best not to be surprised by an auditor asking for that skill. In the world of TV, film, and commercials, auditions happen overnight, and you won't be able to prepare much in the time allotted.

Sports

You must be very proficient in the sport that you say you can play. You don't want to be embarrassed or even fired because you stretched this particular truth. If you haven't played basketball in ten years don't list it. My company was once hired to cast a commercial featuring ice skaters. We had the auditions at an ice rink. When people showed up who had assured us that they could skate, it was obvious that they had exaggerated when they fell flat on their fannies. We were not pleased and called their agents to complain. You really don't want this to happen to you.

Singing

If you are a singer, it should appear not only in special skills but also in the body of your résumé. If on the other hand you sing in the shower or at karaoke, best leave it off. For some reason, many people claim to be singers who, when contrasted with actual singers, fail to impress.

Dance

Ballroom dance comes in very handy in both theatre and film. If you are good at it, be specific. What kind of ballroom? Waltz? Foxtrot? Jitterbug? If you are formally trained as a modern dancer or in ballet or flamenco or other complicated dance forms, it is helpful to include the number of years you have trained, including your general proficiency. Again, if you aren't a dancer, don't say that you are.

Musical instruments

The rule of thumb is that if you haven't played in a year, and if you don't own the instrument that you claim to play, it is best to either leave it off, or to say something like, "trombone in high school band."

Fluency in foreign languages

If you are a native speaker of any language other than English, please indicate this. In general, this is required when you will be broadcasting to native speakers. Don't try to stumble through this unless you are very sure that when native speakers hear you, they believe that you are one as well. If you speak a Mexican dialect of Spanish, or Columbian or some such, including that information may also give you a leg up.

Vehicles

Because TV and commercials often feature people driving various vehicles, licensure is necessary. If you can drive anything other than a standard transmission, that can come in handy. Think of the number of times you see tractors in commercials. I had an actor friend who didn't have a license. He was cast in a commercial where he had to be seen leaving a parking space. He did know how to drive, so it didn't seem to be a problem for him. It wasn't a problem until he hit a crew member standing behind the car as he backed up to leave the space. Luckily no one was hurt, but the actor never worked for that very prominent director again.

Other things NOT to put on a professional acting résumé

- Dates of any kind (dates are reserved for those seeking an academic posting or applying to schools).

- You home phone number or address.

- Tech or directing credits (should be on a separate résumé).

- Statement of purpose: leave that to corporate.

- Your spiritual beliefs have no place on a business document.

11

The Album of Your Life Play:

Pictures, Reels, Websites

Every actor needs pictures. These marketing materials must reveal something that makes an agent, a director, or a casting director want to meet you. It is actually quite simple. A good picture opens doors.

The problem is that there are many opinions on what makes a good picture. The casting directors says, "I want the picture to look like the actor who walks into the studio," the agent says "I want a picture that sells the actor," the actor's mom says, "I want a picture that shows my sweet daughter's lovely face and hair," and the actor says, "I want a picture that pleases everyone including my friends, my teachers, and my zumba coach."

Choosing a picture is an infuriating process for someone entering the profession or trying to restart a career stuck in the theatrical mud. So what does one do? Most people pick up promotional cards attached to the bulletin board at school or scan the "trades" for a photographer whose pictures somehow catch their attention. A smart actor asks their friends in the business, their teachers, or other supposedly knowledgeable people. Those that are naive simply go to the local photography studio. They wear whatever they think makes them look attractive, and two days later receive a picture that will look great in a frame on mom's dresser. Other sadly misled actors bop on down to the mall and have a picture done at Beauty Pix. Or, they have their friend who took a class in photography meet them at a picturesque area and snap away. None of these are professionally advisable.

Good, professional headshot photographers are specialists who study their local market, understand the demands of the business, and who try to capture something that might be useful to the actor. They know the agents, the casting directors, and the theatre people in the cities in which they work. Each city/market has its own style of headshot and the photographer must understand that style. A picture that works in Houston will not work in Chicago or in Los Angeles. There are many bad photographers who believe that they are doing good work, but there are only a few really good and insightful photographers and they charge quite a lot of money for their expertise.

Once you finally choose a photographer, there is usually a meeting to see if you are comfortable with him or her. In this meeting, the photographer will usually quiz you about how you wish to be perceived. They will ask what you think your market is, what you want to convey in the picture, what kind of music you want at the session, and whether you want a make-up/hair artist to take care of your look.

The difficulty with this can be that you might think the photographer will look at you and see that secret ingredient you know is lurking if only someone would look deeply enough. Very few, even the best, can do this. They are working in a two-dimensional format, and unless you are wearing your soul on your face, they will not rescue you. You may desperately wish for the person taking your pictures to tell you what to do, and how you should be marketed. However, without some real input from you, your own individual presence will be lacking. The resulting picture may make you look like a movie star, no flaws, beautiful eyes and hair. It will be the picture your mom will like, you will be flattered by it, and an agent will reluctantly agree to use it. But the casting director won't even turn it over to look at the résumé because the picture is yet another standard photo of an actor with no personality attached.

There are some guidelines you can follow to avoid cashing in all of the savings bonds your grandmother gave to you. Professional headshot photographers all have websites. Go to them and investigate very carefully. Do the pictures displayed make you want to meet the actors pictured in them? Don't worry about how pretty the people look, try to examine whether the photo found something unique in the actor. Notice whether the actors are all in odd positions or closed positions, whether they are all looking up out of the corners of their eyes, or if their pictures are really about a woman's hair. Women in particular need to examine whether the photographer believes that all females need to look sexy even when, in all likelihood, most of us are neither great beauties nor models. Beware of too much skin, or distracting wardrobe that muddies the aim of the picture. Remember the shot must allow someone in the industry to make a guess at how you might be helpful in a project.

Before spending all of your money, do some practice shots with a friend—practice looking into and through the lens, <u>rather than at the camera</u>. Be sure that your shirt, sweater, top is not the most important thing in the picture. You want to appear to have a relationship with the person on the other side of the lens, not allow the camera to take a picture of you. Wear your hair the way you think you will in the actual pix and wear the wardrobe that your are considering using. Often, a shirt that looks great in three dimensions is not two-dimensionally attractive. Beware of drooping necklines and blouses or shirts that stand up on your back even when you adjust them.

Your hair is none of your business! Current very hip styles shouldn't be a choice for you unless you are a model. Do not think that the Mohawk you want to wear for everyday is going to help you get work unless a project is looking specifically for a man wearing a Mohawk. The same is true for facial hair. I know the argument, "Well, I would be willing to shave." However, as a casting director, I wouldn't risk asking an actor to shave for a callback because it would appear as if the project was ready to commit, and no casting person could ever guarantee that if you shaved the producers or directors would like you any better. Having two pictures, one with beard and one without beard, still doesn't actually let anyone know how you actually look.

Now, this rule is very breakable. It depends on several things. First, African American men are pretty much exempt from the no facial hair rule for some unknown reason. Second, if you are Caucasian and decide to keep your beard, you will definitely be the person called whenever a beard is needed. This casting might include bikers, people who watch sports, people doing sports, lowlifes of many varieties, artists (I don't include them in the lowlife category), and someone's brother-in-law.

Specifically for women, you are not your hair. Do not let the stylist or photographer fall in love with it. And, if you feel that you *are* your hair, for Pete's sake, have at least one picture with it out of the way, up on top of your head or in back or whatever. If you decide to dye your hair a completely different color than the color in your pictures, you will either need new pix or you will cause some consternation in the casting department.

Also, if you must wear jewelry, and I don't see why you must, but if you feel it necessary, at least make it something conservative. You want these pictures to last a little while and jewelry fashions change frequently. Don't complain when your casting is limited by your personal cosmetics or taste. Please, no hats, at least not for your first pictures, they look like you are trying way too hard.

For both genders, unless you want to play only slackers and druggies, no nose rings, tongue studs, enormous ear holes, or other such self-mutilating forms of self-expression. Currently, small tattoos, in discrete locations, are all right, but huge ones across your chest, neck, back, arms, or any other major part of your generally visible anatomy, are not a good idea. You may think that writing your life philosophy on your chest is a good idea, but I beg you to reconsider. I don't think this discrimination is a good thing. I don't believe that people who have made these choices are less than good people with ethics and morals like the rest of us. However, the world of theatre and media deals with symbols, and the symbols you apply to your body will send messages to an audience whether you intend it or not. On the other hand, I think that Hamlet with a "Born to Die" tattoo on his forehead might be exciting. However, it would take a rare director to see the value. Again, the rules are not set in stone; you must decide what is of value to you. The first view anyone has of your picture, and often of you, is going to be on a website.

Actors need to remember that we don't see headshots in person anymore . . . They are submitted as a thumbnail picture—so they need nice close-up shots—3/4 shots don't work for online submissions as the heads in them are the size of a thumbtack.
JENNIFER RUDNICKE, casting director

As I have discussed, there are ways to use a picture to suggest casting range in a very broad sense. One of the most important elements is wardrobe that hints at a social, educational, or economic level. Many casting directors in film and TV use a shorthand, describing a character as "upscale casual," or "rural," or "suburban mom," or "artsy type," or "girl next door," or "jock," or "beer babe," or "construction worker," or "athletic," and many other concepts too varied to list. Most of these can be broken down into white collar, blue collar, beer guys and gals, mom, college kid, or young bride/groom. Your picture should probably lean towards one of these. Is your first media job going to be as a fast-food worker, as a young lawyer, a new mother, an artist, or will it be with a group of friends watching a ballgame? Of course, your answer will be "I can do any of these," but the professional casting person will disagree. And as with any part of show business, don't do it if you don't want to, no one is dragging you to the audition.

In any event, you will need new pictures within twelve to eighteen months of your first shots. During that time you will make many discoveries about how show business sees you, and how you can either capitalize on that or change the perception.

Reels

When you do a voiceover, a film, or a commercial, you need a copy of it for your records, because eventually you need to create a reel or a sampling of your work. If it's a voiceover, you may ask the engineer to send you a copy or request one from the producer. For a film or television show, you will have to wait until it is released to record it yourself. However, there are companies who make a living doing what is referred to as "air checks." They do the searching and waiting for you and deliver the scene, or the show, to you in whatever format you desire. They can edit anything you wish as well as making a reel for you, but the expense is not minimal. To find such a company simply Google "film air check." Of course, you could make your own or find a computer-savvy friend who knows how to use a video-editing program such as Final Cut or iMovie. Reels can be simple or full of complex effects. My advice: simple is better. The reel must be structured in such a way that the viewer will continue to watch and

the footage on it must be representative of your work; tha.
is needed.

It is possible to put together a sample of your work in a play or by doing monologues or scenes for camera. (There are copyright issues that need to be addressed concerning the material you choose to do.) I caution you to remember that the reel must look as if it were professionally lit and framed, that your hair and make-up be appropriate for camera, and that you are conservatively cast in whatever you do. It would also not be wrong to hire an acting teacher or a director if you are thinking of doing such a video on your own.

Websites

Once you have a reel, your agent will distribute it to whomever asks to see it, and you can distribute it as well. I think the best place for it is on your personal website. As your career grows you will need one featuring your work (both on-camera and voiceover), your headshots, reviews, and whatever else you find relevant. My belief is that such a webpage is not needed until you have some actual work under your belt, so you might put it off until the third or fourth year of your career. However, if you want to create your own page, check out the pages of other actors to see what you are attracted to and what they include. Your webpage can be very simple or full of bells and whistles, but remember, the page is not there to be admired; it is there to get you hired!

As with your reel, you need not pay tons of money to make a page—there are simple programs available to assist you. As long as the page doesn't look carelessly done, such sites as **www.wordpress. org** and **www.godaddy.com** are perfectly acceptable. (A personal request, please, avoid dark backgrounds with light print, I can barely read them.) Once you have a webpage, it can be linked to others, but your agent will want to be in on such decisions.

12

Learning Your Lines and Showing Up for Your Life Play:

Auditions

It is an unfortunate fact of life that you will have to perform monologues at the beginning of your career. If there were a better way to see lots of actors in a short amount of time, such exercises would not be needed, but so far it is a standard way of doing this job.

In general, actors should have a minimum of four monologues at their command. The basics are: modern dramatic, modern comic, classical dramatic, and classical comic. These designations are guidelines and every theatre and casting office has different understandings of what these labels mean. I will devote some time to each, beginning with the classical.

The reason a theatre asks to see a classical piece is to determine whether you can handle what is called "heightened language." Heightened language is writing that includes strong images, poetic or lyrical language, or extended lines of thought.

The benchmark dramatic classical is Shakespeare, in verse. Comic classical can mean Shakespeare or others of that time period either in verse or prose. Of course, there are other playwrights considered classical, including such figures as Moliere, George Bernard Shaw, Christopher Marlowe, Ben Jonson, or any of the Greek playwrights. But the big kids do the Bard, Shakespeare.

If you are not trained to do Shakespeare or other plays written in verse, either don't do a classical monologue at all, or use one of the other playwrights I have suggested as they tend to be less complex. There is no reason for you to waste both your own and the auditor's time doing something in which you have no confidence. Do not be intimidated by the arbitrary rules. You are at the audition to show what you are good at, not what you have been commanded to do. No one will be mad at you or assign you to a list of actors who are forbidden to appear at their theatre if you stray from the rulebook, unless *all* they do is the Bard.

If you want to do a Shakespearean piece but have not been trained in it, coaches, books, and videos can introduce you to the rudiments. There are keys to understanding the verse (iambic pentameter) that can help you to understand the work more easily and it is actually fun to learn. Some well-meaning people will tell you that you do not need to know verse technique to do the classics, but those people are not hiring actors for money to appear in classical plays. Do not be misled, it is assumed that you must be truthful, but heightened language demands larger truths and requires deeper commitment to language and action than most contemporary dramas.

Some of you will say that you hate Shakespeare, but that is because you have seen some of the really dreadful Shakespeare being done all over the country. If you are one of the confused haters, I suggest that you watch two films: *Henry V* with Kenneth Branagh and then *Richard III* with Ian McKellan. If you still hate Shakespeare, you actually do hate Shakespeare, but once you see the Bard done well, you will probably change your mind.

Modern dramatic and modern comic means anything written in the past ten years. In academia, this may stretch to fifty years or more, but one of the tests of a professional actor is an acquaintance with what is current in the contemporary theatre world. Again, the designation of dramatic and comic need not deter you. In modern literature, most things are a mixture. Comic monologues should not be jokes nor look like stand-up routines, and dramatic pieces do not necessitate weeping. As a matter of fact, actors are the only people I know who work at crying—most of us try diligently to avoid doing so. Tears do not determine the worth of an actor. A good dramatic monologue probably concerns a serious topic being taken seriously, and a good comic monologue probably concerns a trivial topic being taken seriously. Drama generally involves people trying to behave well in difficult situations and comedy often features people behaving badly in absurd situations. Those are just rules of thumb, but they can work.

While you were training, many of you will have done monologues that were hard for you to do or stretched your range, and they are often used as a means of teaching. DO NOT DO THIS FOR THE PROFESSION! Your monologues are a product and they should be so well memorized and easily done that if I were to awaken you in the middle of the night you would do them as beautifully as if you had time to prepare.

Another mistake beginning actors make is to learn a monologue the week or even the day that it is to be presented. What a bad idea! Doing this is self-sabotage. The situations in which monologues are done are so nerve-wracking that anything not deeply embedded in the actor's body and brain will in most cases desert them. There will be times when a theatre asks for a piece to be prepared from the play they are doing, but at that time all of the actors auditioning will be at the same disadvantage.

In creating your menu of monologues, it is important that they contrast with one another. A formula for this is to ensure that each monologue is delivered to a different relationship. If all of your pieces are to a lover, your choices of behavior will be limited. Find one piece to a lover, one to a sibling, one to a parental figure, and one to a child. It is best to stick to these sorts of essential relationships because they have the most deeply felt connections for an actor.

Most theatres ask that monologues be sixty or ninety seconds; stay within these guidelines. Many of you will say that this is too short a time, but remember, the auditors are not there to hear the story; they are there to see you. It is highly likely that they know the monologue you are delivering even if you think it is obscure. If you are skillful, your potential and talent can be seen in five seconds.

What does that mean for you? Your monologue must begin well and not be dependent on a lot of exposition. The opening line must excite attention. Good writing is essential in this situation. There are so many pieces that begin with cliché lines such as "I remember when I was a boy" that are not at all helpful. Make sure that the first line you utter has some juice in it.

Once you have determined the monologues you are going to use, drill and drill and drill the text. You don't have to act them fully every day, but you do need to keep the words flowing. Do them in your car, while you run in the park, while you wash dishes, and anytime you have a free minute. You should be able to do a sixty-second piece in thirty seconds of rapid-fire motor-mouth.

Among your pieces, there will be one that I call your "signature" piece. This choice should be in your age range and obvious casting range. Generally this is the modern dramatic, but it might be the modern comic. All of the others should contrast to it. You should love it and love doing it. If not, you will bore yourself and the auditors as well.

To find material, you must as usual do your research. It is a good idea to read the arts sections of the *New York Times*, *Chicago Tribune*, and the *Los Angeles Times* where new plays will be discussed and reviewed. Make it a habit to attend any new plays in your vicinity. There are also many online sites where new playwrights' organizations feature their plays, and the website Doolee.com can help you to discover new plays as well.

Monologue presentation and selection

Some of this may contradict what your teachers have told you. If your teacher is someone who directs or casts professionally, listen to him or her on this matter; there are regional differences in everything. If not, use these words of wisdom.

- A monologue is a piece of a play where you are talking to someone else. The auditor is metaphorically between the two of you.

- Doing a monologue may feel artificial, but remember that when you are on your cellphone you don't see the person to whom you are speaking and yet you have ideas and reactions based on your knowledge of that person. If I watch you on your phone, it looks like an interrupted monologue.

- Pick pieces where you are a winner, where you are actively trying to change someone.

- Avoid pieces in which you are a victim or a whiner. Many actors choose "poor me" speeches because they allow them to demonstrate their ability to cry. After twenty of these sorts of self-flagellations, most directors and casting directors will be driven to tears themselves.

- If you are angry in the speech, make sure you are not simply annoyed but *really* angry. If you are joyful, do it. In-betweens are not all that interesting.

- Always do any piece from a righteous point of view; do not indict the character that you are portraying even if he or she is the villain of the play.

- Never do anything without endowing the role with a sense of humor. I don't mean comedy, I mean the sort of sense of humor that in life we bring to the most serious of situations, such as wit, irony, self-deprecation, or simply a way of not taking oneself too seriously. We do this in life and therefore eliminating it from a dramatic speech makes you seem unintelligent and self-pitying.

- Never play beneath your own intelligence. Even a person or character who appears to be less that intellectually gifted is frantically trying to figure things out.

- Never do a monologue in a dialect unless it is requested.

- Standing stock still staring forward unwaveringly is not the best way to do your presentation. You don't have to rush around the stage, but movement is not against the law and can actually help you to structure your monologue.

- Place the person to whom you are speaking slightly above the auditor's heads.

- Do not do both of your monologues in the same geographical place in the same geographical way. If you have done the first one directly to the front, do the second slightly to the right or left of the auditors.

- For stage, never talk to a chair or to the auditor. In Los Angeles there will be film casting directors who ask you to talk directly to them, but for stage this is not a good idea.

- Never use props, fake them. I know, I know, you really need the book or the drink or whatever, but you will drop it, spill it, forget it, or it will break. As with everything, you can break this rule, but know that you are doing so and guard against the problems. I once had an actor come to an audition carrying a typewriter, a typing table, and paper. It took him five minutes to set up and to my recollection he never used them. What was wrong with his idea? He thought that I wanted to see the play and that he needed tremendous support to perform his overly long speech. For him, acting was a very difficult thing to do, and as a casting director, I want actors who act easily.

- Avoid speeches with bodily fluids.

- Keep your clothes on.

- Unless it is requested, don't do a piece from the play being auditioned. If you are so excited about being in that particular production and have the time, do a piece by the same author.

- While it is not usual, there are actors who can write their own speeches. You'd best be a pretty great writer to do this, but I have known actors who have carried it off successfully. The only caution is to make up the name of the play and playwright and NEVER reveal that it was your own endeavor.

- An addendum to the prior advice; in many of the monologue classes I have taught, there have been actor/playwrights who have written pieces for their classmates. Again, title and playwright should not reveal the origin of the speech.

- It is not wrong to find a monologue in a novel or a short story and to craft it for the stage yourself, but you should be careful that the "literary-ness" of it is removed.

- If you have an obviously non-Caucasian background, make sure that one of your pieces reflects that heritage.

- Don't wear anything that calls attention to the garment itself, especially very short skirts, tight clothes or interesting shoes.

Ladies, just wear simple, low-heeled pumps. Women's shoes are the most often ridiculed in a roomful of casting people, followed only by low-cut, tight sweaters. You want to be seen as an actor, not as a potential bedmate.

- While your clothes should be simple that does not mean that bright colors are forbidden. We see so many actors wearing black clothes that a burst of color can actually wake an auditor up. Also on that subject, try not to dress as if you are applying for a job in a bank. Look like the actor you are. Shirts and ties are not needed; casual, clean, well fitting clothes are all that is.

- Do not expect to be introduced to the auditors. Sometimes this will happen and sometimes it won't. Don't run around trying to shake hands.

- Expect to be messed over. Expect the auditors to keep you waiting, or for them to be eating, or to be rude, or to not be there, or to interrupt you, or for a buzz-saw to be going on directly behind you, or for your shoes to fall apart, or for a bug to fly up your nose (all taken from actual case studies). *It is best to expect the worst because then the best is far more than could be imagined and the worst is rarely as bad as one could conceive* (from a play entitled *Under the Sycamore Tree* by Sam and Bella Spewack).

- Stop complaining when the worst happens, it is only to be expected.

- All is fair in love and monologues. Many people will tell you the rules, but the best advice is to do the thing that you must do to reveal your acting ability. Find a way to act that allows you to act and disregard the rules.

Prepared scenes

In Los Angeles, it is likely that you will be asked to do a prepared scene for a casting director, although there are still those who will ask for a monologue. Most of the same rules apply.

You should have two scenes ready to perform, one for sitcom and one for dramatic series. These scenes can be chosen from plays or from screenplays. If you use a play, be sure that it is not overly verbose. If you use a screenplay, be careful that it is not something extraordinarily famous. You don't want your scene compared to the one that Meryl Streep did as a young woman. The scenes you choose should be balanced for you and your partner because whether you like it or not an audition of this sort is an audition for both of you. (It is difficult to find another actor who agrees to "not perform" in a scene because it is your audition.) A rule of thumb is to avoid partners who would compete with you for roles in age or gender. So, someone of the opposite sex, or someone who plays someone older than you, is ideal. The scene should be no longer than four minutes and it is wise to avoid doing the most dramatic scene of the play.

Again, the auditors are not interested in the story, they are looking to see if you can be in the moment and respond honestly to your partner. They do not need to see every note that you are capable of playing. They do need truthful behavior in a realistic setting. Speaking of settings, these scenes are often done in a small office, so it is best to keep the staging to a minimum and avoid props or other things that might backfire. And as with monologues, no bodily fluids or nudity please.

Once you have found the scene you are going to do, drill, drill, drill the lines so that both of you are so secure nothing can rattle you. It is a good idea to videotape the scene to determine whether it is camera-size. People in Hollywood do not believe the adage that you can always bring a performance down to size. They tend to be on the conservative edge of that argument.

If the auditor asks you to do the scene again and gives you adjustments, it doesn't mean that they think you are wrong or untalented or anything of that nature. It means that they think you are worth taking time to investigate and to determine whether you are able to take direction. You have actually stirred up some interest! When you are given any new direction, listen closely, and if need be, reiterate what has been said. It is often just at this moment that actors either nod enthusiastically and do the same thing they did before the new direction, or defend themselves saying something like, "Well that isn't what my famous teacher said." Perfectly sane individuals, who are good actors, will say and do things they would never say or do if they were in their right minds. Always be on the look-out for self-sabotage!

Casting people tend to keep poker faces and will rarely tell you how they feel about your performance. Do not expect feedback. You will know how you did when you are called in for a reading. Even if you are not called in, it may be that the casting person has no script suitable for you, or got sick, or is no longer in the business, or hates people from Des Moines, or simply has no taste.

Finally, concerning both forms of prepared auditions, keep a sense of humor about yourself, and the silly situations actors are forced to endure. You will survive to act another day. It is rare for anyone but you to remember you at all unless you were either wonderful or dreadful. Remember that you are not the center of the auditor's world and that they will see many more people before you come around again. In all likelihood, unless you were shockingly bad or stupid or rude, they will have forgotten all about you. An actor has many lives; nothing is final.

13

The Location of Your Life Play:

Markets

This chapter is intended to acquaint you with cities in which you might stand a chance of working as a newcomer, where you might make some interesting theatre. Some of them are places to put down roots, some are simply there to build your acting chops and hopefully put some things on your résumé that might count when and if you move. As I worked through which cities to include, it became pretty obvious that most of the work (with a few notable exceptions) was centered in regions on the east of the Mississippi River. Some of the markets to which I refer stand alone and don't interconnect with others, artistically or geographically. Chicago, New York, Los Angeles, and Minneapolis are pretty much what they are. Actors from those places don't often drive to auditions nearby, as actors in the Chesapeake Bay area might do. Oddly enough, the actors in Austin, Texas seem to move back and forth to New Orleans rather often, and actors in New Orleans are well known in Atlanta. Actors in Philadelphia connect to New York and Pittsburgh. The number of actors on buses, trains, and highways on any given day must be pretty high in certain areas of the country.

I had wanted to be very formulaic in constructing these databases, the same data covered in each city, but as I moved ahead, I realized that each place was different, my knowledge of each place was different, and the values in each market were different. For instance,

I don't see much to be gained by giving you a list of Los Angeles theatres—that is not what Los Angeles does. Certainly you will work in theatre there if you go; I did, but the focus is movies.

I had intended to include New Orleans as a place for actors to live and love. The city is a real playground, but it doesn't support the arts very much and there is not a lot for performers to do. Recently, owing to the state's funding of film companies, many filmmakers have been shooting there, not only because it is cheap, but also because everyone loves its seductive culture. The arts flourish, just not theatre. I spent some time there, did a teeny, tiny film role in the French Market, and hoped to find a way to encourage you to investigate it. But finally I can't recommend it as a place to begin a career unless you get really lucky.

When I do the next edition of this book, I want to include Seattle, WA, Portland, Oregon, some places in Arizona and New Mexico, as well as San Francisco. However, this book is long enough and I think that if you notice what it is that I have done, you can investigate on your own. The web is a great leveler! I apologize in advance if your favorite city or theatre has not been included.

In determining what agencies, what theatres, what teachers, and so forth would be listed and which were excluded I interviewed people in the markets where I hadn't lived and worked, read the blogs and websites about the industry in each city, and sometimes dug deeper to make sure that I wasn't suggesting that you connect with unsavory types lying in wait for hopeful artists. If you find that I have inadvertently done so, please let me know through the website maintained by Methuen Press for actors and theatre folks. You will find some blogs there from me as well.

Chicago: City of Big Shoulders, the Windy City, the Second City

The Chicago market is a vibrant, cultured, and attractive place for actors and other artists in which to live and work. Many of you would not be happy there because of the cold winters and hot summers. For hardier folks, the beauty of Lake Michigan and its beaches, the wonderful fall and spring seasons, and the many unique neighborhoods that give Chicago its "down home" feel are worth the snow and mosquitoes. Many people believe that Chicago is a dangerous place to live, however, its violent crime rate is about the same as New York City and Los Angeles, with most of the crime confined to the south and west portions of the city proper. Actors tend to live on the relatively safe north and east sides.

Compared to Los Angeles or New York, Chicago is a fairly inexpensive place in which to live; housing is plentiful, an average apartment is large for the money, a car is not needed, and public transportation is safe and easily available.[5] A monthly, unlimited-ride transit card in Chicago for bus and subway (the "El") costs $100. The same deal in New York is $112. In Los Angeles there is a transit system, however, for most actors, it is not adequate. I haven't been able to pin down an average amount for car ownership and maintenance in Los Angeles but you need a car to get to auditions, which can be spread out over a very large area.

Housing in New York is 181 percent more expensive than Chicago and overall expenses in the Big Apple are 62 percent higher than in Chicago. In Los Angeles, living expenses are 58 percent higher and housing is 187 percent higher. Apartment rental in Chicago for a one bedroom averages $1,000, two bedrooms, $1,200.

The percentage of people employed in the arts in the Windy City is 2.85 as opposed to the nationwide average of 1.88, and the yearly per capita average income for actors is $28,202. Additionally, because

---

[5] http://www.bestplaces.net/: Sperling's Best Places. This compilation of data is based not only on federal and state studies, but also on social indicatiors such as number of sports teams, and so forth.

Chicago is the third largest population center in the United States, and because it has a diversified economy, day jobs are not difficult to find.

Insofar as "show business" is concerned, agents and casting directors are very accessible. There are approximately twenty talent agencies and five active casting agencies, most of whom handle TV, film, commercials, and other on-camera work. A few are dedicated to voiceover only. Most do some casting for theatre, but in general theatre casting is done by the theatre itself. Theatres have general auditions as well as auditions that are usually announced online for any shows being cast. Many theatres are based in a "company" way of doing business rather than a "producers" concept having been originally formed by a group of actors.

In addition to the myriads of commercials and independent films being shot daily in Chicago, TV series set in Chicago during 2013 included *Betrayal* (ABC), *Chicago Fire* (NBC), *Chicago PD* (NBC), *Crisis* (NBC), *Mind Games* (ABC), and *Sirens* (USA). Studio features filmed in Chicago in 2013 included *Divergent*, *Jupiter Ascending*, and *Transformers 4*. There are also many national searches for pilot season and for specific roles in films and TV series. While the number of films represents a recent reduction in the usual amount, the uptick in TV series offset that loss and actually created more jobs for actors. A new studio complex, Cinespace, is drawing more and more business to town because of its state of the art construction. The same company intends to create a "backlot," much like that maintained by Hollywood studios. While the amount of film and TV work may seem small compared to NYC or LA, looked at from the number of actors needed versus the number of actors in Chicago, the odds are far better than in either of the two larger markets.

A large percentage of adult actors in Chicago are both AEA and SAG/AFTRA, meaning that while neither the AEA nor the SAG figures concerning per capita income look promising, the combining of these income streams is what actually matters. There are approximately 1,600 AEA members and 1,900 SAG members in the city. By and large, Equity actors support themselves through their work as performers. According to actress Linda Gillum:

No one really makes their living just doing only theatre, so we all do something else. This generally means teaching jobs, voiceover and commercial work; and TV and film when they come through town. For a blink-and-you'll-miss-me role on a television show, an actor might get $600 for the day. That's a nice chunk for a single day's work, but those opportunities are few and far between.

There are about thirty Equity theatres in Chicago, and they gather most of their casts in the city itself with supplementary casting done in New York. This tendency is one of the things that most distinguishes the Chicago theatrical scene from smaller markets.

For musical theatre performers, Chicago may not be an ideal place. There are only four theatres that do an almost exclusive diet of musical plays and two of those are in the distant suburbs. A few of the larger theatres produce a musical every so often, but it is not standard fare. When a musical production comes from New York to "sit down" it frequently hires Chicago actors. It is not that there isn't any work, but compared to New York, the pickin's are lean.

It seems as if there is a new theatre born every day, but the number of theatres remains fairly constant at around 300. The non-institutional theatres are called "storefront" theatres because many of them have created theatre spaces in old stores throughout the city. There are also numerous companies who have no established home. These homeless theatres rent spaces at any of several venues provided for that purpose. These small companies are usually non-Equity or they employ a certain number of AEA members mixed with the non-Equity actors. They pay anywhere from nothing to about $400 per week. While actors do not make much money in these companies, they are able to create exciting work and most actors in the city spend a certain amount of time in these groups.

The lists that follow are not complete, nor in any particular order of importance. they are meant to feature top people in their fields. I will continue to do this throughout the market survey.

Top agents: SAG/AFTRA franchised

Stewart Talent
58 W. Huron
Chicago, IL 60610
(312) 943 3131
www.stewarttalent.com
Also New York and Atlanta

Gray Talent Group
727 S. Dearborn Suite 312
Chicago, IL 60605
(312) 666 5404
www.graytalentgroup.com
Also LA and NYC

Unpaid Internships are available

Marissa Paonessa Talent
1512 Fremont #105
Chicago, IL 60642
(773) 360 8749
www.paonessatalent.com

Grossman and Jack Talent
33 W. Grand Avenue, Ste 402
Chicago, IL 60654
(312) 587 1155
www.grossmanjack.com

Management companies

Management companies for actors are a new development in Chicago. Principato-Young, a Los Angeles based company, hired Brook Shoemaker, a former agent, as their Chicago-based representative. Brooke currently freelances and does her own scouting. At present, she doesn't take submissions.

Top independent casting directors

Paskal/Rudnicke Casting
10 W. Hubbard St. Ste#2R
Chicago, IL 60610
(312) 527 0665 *(do not call)*
www.prcasting.com

Full service agency: TV, film, theatre, commercial. Unpaid
internships are available.

Claire Simon Casting
1512 N. Fremont Ste. 204
Chicago, IL 60622
(312) 202 0124 *(do not call)*
www.simoncasting.com

Full service agency: TV, film, theatre, commercial. Unpaid internships
are available.

David O'Connor Casting
1219 W. Madison
Chicago, IL 60607
(312) 226 9112
www.oconnorcasting.tv

Primarily commercial. Unpaid internships are available.

Two Birds Casting
casting@twobirdscasting.com

Strictly theatre at this point.

Marisa Ross Casting
c/o iO Theater
1501 North Kingsbury Street
Chicago, IL 60642
(774) 722 8675
http://marisarosscasting.com

Film and TV.

Top photographers

The individuals are listed in no particular order. All information on pricing is taken directly from the photographer's website and is subject to change.

Brian McConkey Photography
(312) 563 1357
www.brianmcconkeyphotography.com
Three looks $375
Five looks $550
Includes high and low resolution email link of entire shoot. The link is emailed five business days after the day of the shoot. Brian is the go-to guy in Chicago, he understands the business and has been working in the city for quite a long time.

Janna Giacoppo Photography
(312) 437 5555
Studio manager: Julia
www.jannagiacoppo.com
Three looks $550
Three wardrobe changes as well as hair and makeup changes if desired. 300 images shot and copy of ALL images in high-res JPEG format available the same day as the session. Online proof sheets of the entire session (available within two business days).
Two looks $450, 200 images shot, copy, and proofs included.
One look $350, 100 images shot, copy and proofs included. Makeup rates are $140 for women, $100 for men.
Janna is based both in LA and in Chicago, her pictures tend towards the LA look, but also work in Chicago.

Johnny Knight Photography
(773) 368 8707
www.johnnyknightphoto.com
No limit to the number of shots or wardrobe changes. $325 actor/ performer photo shoot package. Two to three hours of shooting, approximate. High resolution images on disc. Proofs posted as a private online gallery.
Fairly new to the headshot world though he has been a professional photographer for quite a long time.

Zoe McKenzie Photography
(773) 852 1189
http://zoemckenziephotography.com
Pricing as of December 2014
Three looks men 18 and over, $460, women 18 and over, $475.

Popio Stumpf Photography
(773) 320 4018
http://popiostumpf.com
Chris Popio
Heather Stumpf
Three to four looks $350 for first-time customers, two to two and a half hours or as long as it takes to get an "awesome" shot. 200–250 shots.
High resolution shots presented to the client on a CD. Hair and make-up: $125 for women, $100 for men and children.

Sally Blood Photography
(312) 788 8838
sallybloodheadshots.com
One look $250, one hour, 80–100 images, high Resolution disk of all shots. Make up and hair.
Numerous Looks $425, two to three hours, 150–200 images. High Resolution Disc of all shots.
Make up and hair.

Ian McLaren Photography
(312) 985 6048
www.ianmclarenphotography.com
Session fee $295. Make-up, additional fee.

Top schools and teachers

Acting Studio Chicago
10 W. Hubbard
Chicago, IL 60601
(312) 527 4566
www.actingstudiochicago.com

The oldest and most successful school in Chicago (I admit it, I founded it, but I sold it long, long ago). The approach used in classes is taken from Michael Shurtleff's book, *Audition*. If you are not familiar with this book, give it a read. It is somewhat dated, but the "guideposts" that Michael formulated are useful for every type of work, and not limited to auditioning. The school offers classes in everything from dialects, voice and movement, to auditioning for small roles in films, to monologues to scene study, to voiceover and every other skill actors need to master.

The Green Shirt Studio
4407 N. Clark St
Chicago, IL 60640
(773) 217 9565
www.greenshirtstudio.com

A Meisner based training program lead by some terrific teachers who teach the Meisner technique wisely. Meisner has the potential to be abusive to an actor but not at The Green Shirt Studio.

The Second City Training Center
1608 N. Wells St
Chicago, IL 60614
(312) 664 3959
secondcity.com/tc

Second City is the home of the art of improvisational acting and the classes there are still some of the best instruction any actor can get. The classes are tiered, some for people interested in studying for fun or for developing confidence, and some for actors seeking professional training. There are classes that concentrate on comedy, and others for actors wishing to learn improvisational techniques in rehearsals. There are classes in writing, directing, music, physical theatre, and a host of other fascinating subjects. As with any school this large, the faculty can vary, but by and large, reports from students are always glowing.

IO! Improv
1501 N. Kingsbury St
Chicago, IL 60642
(312) 929 2401
http://ioimprov.com/chicago

IO (formerly Improv Olympics) was founded by Del Close, one
of the original members of the Second City along with Paul Sills,
Mike Nichols, and Elaine May. This training institution created a
new way of working called "The Harold" which led to long form
improvisational works rather than simply scenes. IO is smaller and
more personal than Second City, and has many successful alumni
in TV and film.

The Actors Gym
Specializing in Circus, Aerial & Performing Arts classes
(847) 328 2795
927 Noyes St
Evanston, IL 60201

The School at Steppenwolf
www.steppenwolf.org/Teach-Learn/School-at-Steppenwolf.
aspx

This ten-week summer program is conducted using the facilities
of The Theatre School at DePaul University. Admittance is by
audition.

The Piven Theatre Workshop
927 Noyes St
Evanston, IL 60201
(847) 866 6597

Another of the Chicago institutions for actor training. The Piven
Theatre workshop includes classes for children and adults, all of
which use theatre games developed by Viola Spolin. Additionally
they perform shows in their own theatre.

Top informational websites

Theatre In Chicago: **www.theatreinchicago.com**
www.theatremania.com

Guide to what's happening right now, reviews and auditions. Lots of information.

Actor's Equity
www.actorsequity.org

Rules, advice, and contract info.

SAG/AFTRA:
www.sagaftra.org

Rules, advice, and contract info.

League of Chicago Theatres
www.chicagoplays.com

A complete list of theatres in Chicago as well as tickets, resources, auditions and more!

Theatermania
www.theatermania.com

This site is a national one, but choosing "Other Cities" can take you directly to Chicago offerings. Theatre reviews, synopses, casts, etc. Also good for discount tickets.

Reel Chicago
http://reelchicago.com

Chicago visual media news: a must for actors wanting to know what's going on and who's doing what. This site is for the industry and about the industry, not necessarily aimed at actors.

The Illinois Film Office
www.illinois.gov/dceo/whyillinois/Film/Pages /default.aspx

A resource for what's doing in film and TV in Chicago. Some casting notices included.

Actor Access
www.actorsaccess.com

This "must have" website features actors' headshots and résumés posted by agents and actors alike. It is a service used by casting people to distribute sides, to schedule, and to browse submissions. For actors, it is a place to post pictures and résumés, read breakdowns of what is casting, to get scripts, to read industry advice, and to find classes and seminars. Embedded in the Access site is a service called "Showfax." You must register.

Casting Networks
http://home.castingnetworks.com

Very much like Actor Access, but aimed specifically at LA. Not used as frequently by Chicago CDs and directors. You must register.

Now Casting
www.nowcasting.com

A site for actors to get info, upload videos, and register headshots and résumés. Similar to Casting Networks and Actor Access. You must register.

Chicago Improv Network
www.chicagoimprov.org
Everything improv in Chicago and elsewhere!

Student film information

The following schools have film departments where undergrad and/
or graduate students make student films.

Columbia College: Film & Video Dept.
(312) 369 6783
filmcasting@colum.edu
Casting: Becca Knights

Northwestern University Department of Radio, TV & Film
Studio 22 produces the majority of the student films and is a
student run production company.
The co-presidents listed in the directory are: Chris Simonson,
christophersimonson2007@u.northwestern.edu and Andy
VanBeek, **andrewvan2007@u.northwestern.edu.**

**The School of the Art Institute Film, Video, New Media &
Animation Department:**
MacLean Building, Rm 512
112 S. Michigan Ave.
(312) 345 3827

Flashpoint Academy
(312) 332 0707
(312) 506 0736
Casting: Killian Heilsberg: **killian.heilsberg@flashpointacademy.com**.

DePaul University
Elliott Lonsdale
(312) 362 6862
ELONSDAL@cdm.depaul.edu

Send headshots and résumés via email or snail mail, or drop
off at 14, E. Jackson Blvd., Chicago, IL, room Lower Level 103a.

Top non-musical theatres

Under full actor's equity contracts

The Goodman Theatre
170 North Dearborn Street
Chicago, IL 60601
(312) 443 3800
www.goodmantheatre.org
Casting director: Adam Belcuore

Casting announced on all major websites and on the theatre's
website. The Goodman casts in NYC as well as Chicago and also
uses agent submissions.

Steppenwolf Theatre
1650 North Halsted Street
Chicago, IL 60614
(312) 335 1650
www.steppenwolf.org
Casting directors: Nick Ward, Jessamyn Fuller

Casting announced on all major websites and on the theatre's
website. Steppenwolf, which is a company-based theatre,
casts in NYC as well as Chicago and also uses agent
submissions.

The Court Theatre
5535 S. Ellis Avenue
Chicago, IL 60637
(773) 753 4472
www.courttheatre.org
Casting director: Cree Rankin

Casting announced on all major websites and on the theatre's
website. The Court casts in NYC as well as Chicago and also uses
agent submissions.

Chicago Shakespeare Theatre
800 East Grand Avenue on Navy Pier
Chicago, IL 60611
(312) 595 5656
www.chicagoshakes.com
Casting director: Bob Mason

Casting announced on all major websites and on the theatre's website.
Chicago Shakespeare Theatre casts in NYC as well as Chicago and
also uses agent submissions.

Victory Gardens Theatre
2433 North Lincoln Avenue
Chicago, IL 60614
(773) 871 3000
www.victorygardens.org

Casting announced on all major websites and on the theatre's website.

Lookingglass Theatre
821 North Michigan Avenue
Chicago, IL 60611
(312) 337 0665
www.lookingglasstheatre.org
Casting: Phil Smith

The theatre uses Now Casting where they offer free submission to
actors wishing to register.

Northlight Theatre
9501 Skokie Blvd
Skokie, IL 60077
(847) 673 6300
www.northlight.org
Casting director: Lynn Baber

Casting announced on all major websites and on the theatre's website.

The Writers Theatre
Casting submissions send to:
Casting Department
Writer's Theatre
321 Park Ave
Glencoe, IL 60022
Administration: (847) 242 6001
www.writerstheatre.org

The Writers Theatre also announces its castings on the Actor's Equity Website as well as the League of Chicago Theatre's website. Currently building a new theatre.

Storefront and smaller theatres

AEA or Limited AEA contracts

The American Theatre Company
1909 West Byron Street
Chicago, Illinois 60613
www.atcweb.org
No official casting director

A Red Orchid Theatre
1531 North Wells Street
Chicago, IL 60610
(312) 943 8722
www.aredorchidtheatre.org
No official casting director

Casting notices posted on website.

Teatro Vista
3712 North Broadway, #275
Chicago, IL 60613
(312) 666 4659
www.teatrovista.org
Dedicated to Hispanic artists
No official casting director

Email your headshot/resume: **casting@TeatroVista.org.** Casting notices posted on website.

The Hypocrites
Performing at:
Den Theatre Mainstage
1329 Milwaukee Ave
Chicago, IL 60622
Casting director: Rob Mclean

Please submit electronically only: **hypocritescasting@gmail.com**

Steep Theatre
1115 W Berwyn Ave
Chicago, IL 60640
(773) 649 3186
www.steeptheatre.com
Casting director: Caroline Neff
Predominantly new works

Timeline Theatre Company
615 W. Wellington Ave.
Chicago, IL 60657
(773) 281 8463 (TIME)
No specific casting director
Devoted to works about history

Snail mail submissions only.

Redtwist Theatre
1044 West Bryn Mawr
Chicago, IL 60660
(773) 728 7529
www.redtwist.org
Casting director: Catherine Miller

Profiles Theatre
4147 North Broadway
Chicago, IL 60613
(773) 549 1815
www.profilestheatre.org
No official casting director

Rivendell Theatre Ensemble
5775 North Ridge Avenue #1
Chicago, IL 60660
(773) 334 7728
www.rivendelltheatre.net
No official casting director

Strawdog Theatre Company
3829 North Broadway
Chicago, IL
(773) 528 9696
www.strawdog.org
Casting director: Casey Cunningham

The House Theatre of Chicago
Chopin Theatre
1543 West Division Street
Chicago, IL 60622
(773) 278 1500
www.thehousetheatre.com
Casting director: Marika Mashburn

Please submit electronically: **casting@thehousetheatre.com**

The Neo-Futurists
5135 N. Ashland Ave
Chicago, IL
(773) 878 4557
http://neofuturists.org
No specific casting director
A collective of artists

Casting done through classes and workshops.

American Blues Theatre
Performances at:
Greenhouse Theatre Space
2257 North Lincoln Avenue
Chicago, IL 60613
Mailing address:
1016 N. Dearborn Ave
Chicago, IL.60610
(312) 725 4228
No specific casting director

Email headshots and résumés to: **info@americanbluestheater.com**

Remy Bumppo Theatre
Performances at:
Greenhouse Theatre Space
2257 North Lincoln Avenue
Chicago, IL 60614
Mailing address:
3717 N. Ravenswood Ave Suite 245
Chicago, IL 60613
Casting director: Linda Gillum

Snail mail submissions only. Use Attn: casting at the Ravenswood address.

Jackalope Theatre
1106 West Thorndale Avenue
Chicago, IL 60660
(773) 340 2543
http://jackalopetheatre.org
Mailing address
Jackalope Theatre Co.
5857 N. Kenmore Ave Suite #3
Chicago IL 60660
Casting director: Elana Boulos

The Griffin Theatre
Perform at various venues
Mailing address
3711 N Ravenswood Ave #145
Chicago, IL 60613
(773) 769 2228
http://griffintheatre.com
No specific casting director
Produce both adult and children's shows
Building a new space

Auditions announced on website, Facebook, and the usual websites.

Improv theatres

Casting generally announced on home websites and on the Chicago Improv network (listed in websites).

The Second City
1616 North Wells St
Chicago, IL 60614
(312) 337 3992
www.secondcity.com

Second City holds general auditions approximately once a year and posts them on its website as well as sending out information to its graduates, and comedy and improvisation schools in Chicago. To be considered for an audition, actors must have graduated from a one year program in the study of improvisation (i.e. The Second City Conservatory, iO, The Annoyance or UCB).

The ComedySportz Theatre
929 West Belmont
Chicago, IL
(773) 549 8080
www.comedysportzchicago.com

Casting generally through the school and workshops.

IO! Improv
1501 N Kingsbury St
Chicago, IL 60642
(312) 929 2401
http://ioimprov.com/chicago

Casting generally through the school and workshops.

Annoyance Theatre
4830 North Broadway
Chicago, IL 60640
(773) 561 4665
www.annoyanceproductions.com

Casting generally through the school and workshops.

Musical theatres

Drury Lane Oakbrook Terrace
100 Drury Ln
Oakbrook Terrace
Oakbrook, IL
(630) 530 0111
drurylaneoakbrook.com
No specific casting director

Audition information on website through audition inquiry form,
http://drurylaneoakbrook.com/facility/contact-us/auditions/
and on: **ActorsEquity.org, theatreinchicago.com, playbill.com,
broadwayworld.com**

Marriott Theatre in Lincolnshire
10 Marriott Dr
Lincolnshire, IL
(847) 634 0200
marriotttheatre.com

Send P&R to: Peter Sullivan. Auditions announced on Facebook site
and Twitter.

Marriott Theatre Rehearsal Warehouse
1342 Barclay Blvd
Buffalo Grove, IL 60089

Porchlight Music Theatre
4200 West Diversey Avenue
Chicago, IL 60639
(773) 777 9884
porchlightmusictheatre.org
Casting associate: Rob Lindley

Audition information on website.

Specialty theatres

Redmoon Theatre
Spectacle, Circus, Clown
1463 West Hubbard Street
Chicago, IL 60622
(312) 850 8440
www.redmoon.org
No specific casting director

The Black Ensemble Theatre
4450 N. Clark St
Chicago, IL 60640
www.blackensembletheater.org
No specific casting director
African American artists with a focus on musical greats

Babes With Blades
(773) 904 0391
Performs at various venues
All female combat-oriented theatre

Submit P&R to: **Spark@babeswithblades.com**

Emerald City-Theatre
Children's Theatre
Offices: 2936 N. Southport Ave, 3rd floor
Chicago, IL 6065 (773) 529 2690
Casting email: **casting@emeraldcitytheatre.com**

Performances at various venues.

Links Hall
3111 North Western Ave.
Chicago, IL 60618
(773) 281 0824

An incubation space for performance artists and physical theatre.

Minneapolis and St Paul, Minnesota: lovers of the arts in the Land o' Lakes

For those whose acquaintance with the Twin Cities (TC's) of Minneapolis and St. Paul, Minnesota, centers around the movie *Fargo* and Public Radio's *Prairie Home Companion*, the reality will be quite a revelation. The cities will be found in the top ten of many quality of life surveys. Minneapolis and St. Paul are fertile ground for all of the plastic and performing arts to germinate and grow. Winter weather can be harsh, but it is so much a part of Minnesota life that if you are robust enough it can be a joy. Activity doesn't stop because of the snow. Summer is a time to take advantage of the beautiful parks and lakes within the cities themselves.

Apartment rentals have risen over the last few years, which is not to say that affordable housing is impossible to find. There are lots of options depending on what kind of apartment is comfortable for you: old or new, city or suburbs, access to public transportation or using your car. Of course, having a car can be very convenient, however Metro Transit provides an extensive bus system, there is an expanding light rail, and a very useful website to plan journeys around the TC's without a car. Finding a full two- or three-bedroom house with roommates can bring your monthly rent down to very acceptable levels.

Most of the TC's neighborhoods are safe, but as with all sizeable cities, when looking for safe places, the police departments in both cities publish maps and crime statistics, which will help you to conduct an informed search.

This vibrant community is not a place for actors who wish to become stars, but it is very possible to make a living as an actor in the TC's, building on many opportunities, and to have a satisfying private life as well.

The TC's has an enviable number of live theatres, many performing under Equity contracts of various levels. In addition, there are scores of non-Equity theatres, some of which offer stipends or weekly salaries. Most of these organizations seek actors locally with supplementary casting done outside the state.

In recent years, attracting large-scale film production to Minnesota has faltered. The culprit? More and more states are offering tax incentives (an idea pioneered by Minnesota) to lure moviemakers. Things have begun to turn around; in the meantime there are other opportunities presented by cable channels and independent and student moviemakers. Minnesota's video production is impressive: the fourth largest in the nation. Commercials, industrials, and training films all need actors. To track this work visit the Minnesota Film and TV Board website: **https://mnfilmtv.org**.

The TC's have several well-regarded SAG-AFTRA franchised talent agencies all of whom have a good deal of experience in all aspects of the business. There is also a good non-union agency in town. These agencies generally don't become involved in live theatre casting, because their bread and butter is made primarily in commercials, voiceovers, print, and any film work that happens to be in town. They are also frequently contacted by out of town casting directors to put people on tape because of the high quality of TC's actors.

With so much production, the number of talent agencies and casting directors has risen from one agency in 1958 to thirty or more today, and half a dozen casting offices. Most agencies are not seeking exclusive talent, so you can register with more than one.

A metropolitan area of this size has lots of work for actors to wait tables, but other day jobs are numerous:

- Theme parks and festivals including Nickelodeon Universe at Mall of America, Renaissance Festival and Valley Fair in Shakopee, MN.

- Tours to schools including Climb Theatre (**climb.org**) and GTC Dramatic Dialogues (**gtcdrama.com**).

- Minnesota History Center guides, interpreters, history players (**mnhs.org**).

- Crisis Company (**crisiscompany.com**) hires actors to role-play for crisis intervention professionals such as police officers, dispatchers, hospital staff, etc.

- At the University of Minnesota actors role-play as patients to teach doctor/patient interaction and as clients and witnesses for law school students. Both are provided and trained by the Standardized Patient (SP) Program at the University of Minnesota Medical School, **www.ahcsimcenter.umn.edu/ StandardizedPatients/index.htm**.

- The Mayo Clinic in Rochester (an hour and a half by car) also uses SPs.

Top non-musical theaters

The Guthrie Theatre
818 South Second Street
Minneapolis, MN 55415
(612) 377 2224
www.guthrietheater.org

Submit P&R via regular mail to: John Miller-Stephany, associate artistic director, at the above address. General auditions are usually scheduled in the spring. Local auditions for specific shows are listed at: **www.minnesotaplaylist.com**

Jungle Theater
2951 Lyndale Avenue South
Minneapolis, MN 55408
(612) 822 7063
www.jungletheater

Audition notices are found on the AEA hotline, in the *Star Tribune* on the *Star Tribune* website, at **mnplaylist.com**, and on the Jungle's 24/7 audition hotline at (612) 278 0156.

Mixed Blood Theater
1501 S. 4th St
Minneapolis MN 55454
(612) 338 6131
www.mixedblood.com

Send P&R to Jack Reuler, artistic director, at the above address. Formal auditions are conducted annually via the TC Unified Theatre Auditions, as well as periodically for specific shows.

Park Square Theatre
Historic Hamm Building
20 W. 7th Place
St. Paul, MN 55102
(651) 291 7005
www.parksquaretheatre.org

Auditions are posted on the website and **minnesotaplaylist.com**

History Theatre
30 E. 10th St.
St. Paul, MN 55101
(651) 292 4323
www.historytheatre.com

Auditions posted on the theater's website.

Children's Theatre Company
2400 – Third Avenue South
Minneapolis, MN 55404
(612) 874 0400
www.childrenstheatre.org

Auditions posted in *Pioneer Press*, *Star Tribune* and at their website.

Illusion Theater
528 Hennepin Avenue
Suite 704
Minneapolis, MN 55403
(612) 339 4944
www.illusiontheater.org

Submit P&R to the above address. Auditions by invitation only or posted in the *Star Tribune* and on **minnesotaplaylist.com**

The Old Log Theatre
5185 Meadville St.
Greenwood, MN 55331
(952) 474 5951
www.oldlog.com

Send P&R attention R. Kent Knutson. You can also send them via email to **kent.knutson@oldlog.com**. Auditions posted at **Minnesotaplaylist.com**.

Ten Thousand Things Theater
3153 36th Avenue South
Minneapolis, MN 55406
(612) 203 9502
www.tenthousandthings.org

Auditions posted on social media, **minnesotaplaylist.com**, **backstage.com**, and **www.broadwayworld.com**.

The Frank Theatre
3156 23rd Ave S.
Minneapolis, MN 55407-1907
(612) 724 3760
www.franktheatre.org

The Frank participates in the GVPTA's Unified General Auditions. Electronic submissions may be sent to **info@thefranktheatre.com**. Please keep file sizes to under 100K.

Pillsbury House Theatre
3501 Chicago Avenue South
Minneapolis, MN 55407
(612) 825 0459
http://pillsburyhousetheatre.org

General auditions and auditions for specific productions for
both Equity and non-Equity members are held each year.
Send P&R in a Word or a PDF format as one attachment to
pricef@pillsburyhousetheatre.org. Headshots should be 300 dpi,
and your name must appear on your picture. To submit a hard copy,
send your headshot and résumé to attention Faye Price, at the
above address. Actors based in the TC area should make a habit
of checking online at **www.minnesotaplaylist.com**.

The Playwright's Center
Playwrights' Center
2301 East Franklin Avenue Minneapolis, MN 55406
(612) 332 7481
https://pwcenter.org

Casts over 300 roles a year for staged readings of new plays with
Equity and non-Equity actors.
General auditions held once a year in late summer. Dates and
details posted Minnesota Playlist.
For questions about auditions, contact artistic administrator Amanda
Robbins-Butcher at **amandar@pwcenter.org**.

Daytrippers
9152 Old Cedar Ave.
Bloomington MN 55425
(952) 393 3644
www.daytripshows.com

Daytime dinner theater, yum. Auditions posted at
minnesotaplaylist.com

Improv Theatre
Brave New Workshop
824 Hennepin Avenue
Minneapolis, MN 55403
(612) 332 6620
www.bravenewworkshop.com

Shows cast through classes at BNW Student Union or snail mail
P&R to Katy McEwan at the theatre's address.

Musical theater

Theater Latté Da
345 13th Ave NE
Minneapolis, MN
(612) 339 3003
www.theaterlatteda.com

Auditions are posted on **minnesotaplaylist.com**

Chanhassen Dinner Theatres
501 West 78th Street
Chanhassen, MN 55317
www.chanhassendt.com

Auditions posted at the website or **minnesotaplaylist.com.** Auditions
are held for both union and non-union actors a few months prior to
each CDT production.

Nautilus Music Theatre
308 Prince Street #250
Saint Paul, MN 55101
(651) 298 9913
ben@nautilusmusictheater.org
Development of new operas and other forms of music-theatre

Auditions posted on **minnesotaplaylist.com** and on facebook.

Specialty theaters

Dark and Stormy Productions
P.O. Box 6488
Minneapolis, MN 55406
http://www.darkstormy.org

Site-specific productions.

Climb Theatre
6415 Carmen Ave E
Inver Grove Heights, MN 55076
(651) 453 9275
www.climb.org

School tours throughout the upper Midwest. Résumés and headshots are accepted, primarily by email, on a year-round basis. Actor candidates may be invited to audition individually, based on the materials received. Actors may also audition for CLIMB at the TC Unified Theatre Auditions.

Union talent agencies

Wehmann Models/Talent Inc
1128 Harmon Pl.
Minneapolis, MN 55403
(612) 333 6393
www.wehmann.com

Submit P&R and/or voiceover demo by snail mail to agency's address or online via their website.

Moore Creative Talent
3130 Excelsior Blvd
Minneapolis, MN 55416
(612) 827 3823
www.mooretalent.com

The oldest and still most respected agency in the TC. Snail mail
P&R and/or voiceover demo to agency address, no emails.
Call (612) 827 3200 for more information.

The Agency: Model and Talent
700 Washington Ave N.
Suite 210
Minneapolis, MN 55401
(612) 664 1174
http://agencymodelsandtalent.com

Voice Box
210 N. 2nd St. Ste 50
Minneapolis, MN 55401
(612) 367 4119
www.voiceboxtalent.com

Audition procedure on website.

Non-union talent agencies

Nuts Limited
820 Lilac Dr N. St 101,
Minneapolis, MN 55422
(763) 529 0330
nutsltd.com

Submit P&R and/or voiceover demo by mail to agency's address.

Talent Poole
1595 Shelby Ave
Suite 200, The Park Building
St. Paul, MN 55104
(651) 645 2516
talentpoole.com

Submit P&R materials on their website under "New Talent
Submission."

Casting directors

A&E Casting
681 17th Avenue NE, #202,
Minneapolis, MN 55413
(612) 310 5333 (no talent calls)
www.aandecasting.com

All talent must submit electronic P&R to **Toni@aandecasting.com**.
No mail submissions.

Bab's Casting
Barbara Shelton
2637 27th Ave S.
Mpls, Mn.55406
(612) 332 6858
www.babscasting.com

JR Casting
Jean Rohn
400 First Ave N, Suite 515
Minneapolis, MN 55344
(612) 396 9043
www.jrcasting.net

No calls, please. Send electronic P&R to: **jrcastingtoo@q.com**

Lynn Steele Casting
4905 Abbott Ave. S.
Minneapolis, MN 55410
(612) 924 9269
www.steelecasting.com

Submit electronic P&R to **steele@bitstream.net**.

Lynn Blumenthal Casting
401 North Third Street, Suite 660
Minneapolis, MN 55401
(612) 338 0369
www.lbcasting.com

Email P&R to: **office@lbcasting.com**, or snail mail to agency's address.

Samaritan Casting
Minneapolis, MN 55401.
(612) 787 2278
www.samaritancasting.com

Predominantly extras casting. Free posting of actor headshots. Sign up at the website to get sent casting notices at no charge.

Photographers

Dani Werner
(651) 776 7614
www.daniphoto.com
Up to 3 Hours $350.00
Includes:

- A dvd of all images taken during the shoot.

- Full usage rights to all images.

- Online viewing of Dani's top edit.

- Two to three wardrobe changes.

- Two to three background changes.

- Up to four images of your choice retouched.

Craig VanDerSchaegen
(612) 245 8389
www.cvheadshots.com
$300 for two hours
$550 for four hours (and multiple setups)

- Online proof gallery.

- Retouched images.

- 8 x 10 headshot design and layout (if needed).

- Download of optimized images and print-ready files.

Sarah Morreim
(651) 592 8314
www.smorreimphotography.com
$200–330 for one-, two- or three-hour session

- Online proof gallery.

- Proof CD.

- One, two or three professionally retouched hi-res image on CD.

Erika Ludwig
erikaludwigphotography.com

$300 for session with multiple clothing changes. Mini sessions are offered monthly through the Meredith Agency and the Wehmann Agency at reduced rates.

Classes

The Performance Studio
(818) 997 6740 (office)
www.SKHperformancestudio.com

Sandra Horner, who graduated from the Yale School of Drama, has experience in all media as an actress, director, playwright, and teacher. Her teaching is Stanislavski-based using both Meisner and Bobby Lewis training. Her school is also one of the few to offer productions open to the public and the profession.

Michelle Hutchison
401 North Third Street, Suite 660
Minneapolis, MN 55401
(612) 338 0369
www.michellelhutchison.com

A wonderful actress who knows what it's all about. She teaches an excellent on-camera workshop through Lynn Blumenthal Casting. Also available for private coaching.

Barbara Shelton
(612) 332 6858
www.babscasting.com

Babs offers both an "Introduction to the Twin Cities Show Business" and advanced camera classes focused on film, TV, and commercials as well as the biz.

Cheryl Moore Brinkley
(763) 560 5081
www.bvocal.net

Cheryl is a personal voiceover coach and a sought-after actress in the TC. She is a deeply caring and professional teacher whose classes are highly recommended.

Voice Results (Sarah Jones-Larson)
(612) 836 8869
www.voiceresults.com

Voiceover classes and workshops. Great group of professional teachers with a wealth of experience offering wonderful practical classes as well as advice on everything from grooming to making a reel. The classes are a bit more expensive than others but the quality and the attention to detail is extremely impressive.

Beth Chaplin
Contact through NUTS (Non Union Talent Agency)
(763) 529 0330

One of the most knowledgeable actors in the TC. Beth knows everyone and has an encyclopedic understanding of how the TCs work. She teaches classes in ear prompter technique as well as other necessary skills. Beth is a working actor, dedicated teacher and caring person.

The Guthrie
(612) 347 1197
www.guthrietheater.org

While the Big G, as it is often called, is the biggest fish in town for theatre, its classes are relatively low impact for professional actors. Perhaps this is because the teachers are all actors who are in production most of the time. Reviews are very mixed between ecstatic and ho-hum. Some of the actors can teach and some can't. However, when you get a good teacher, you're likely to be very, very happy. If you're lucky enough to get any of them, Raye Birk is a dream of a teacher, as are David Mann, and Candace Barrett.

Brave New Institute Student Union
(612) 377 8445
www.bravenewworkshop.com
John Sweeney, producer and owner extraordinaire
Jeni Liledahl, teacher without equal

The Brave New Workshop has been a Minneapolis institution since 1958. It has spawned many notable TV and film performers and writers. Improvisation is essential training for all actors and the Brave New Institute provides some of the best training in the country.

Robert Rosen
(612) 251 4456
www.robertsrosen.com
rr@robertsrosen.com

Improvising and devising. Robert Rosen has all of the right stuff to teach you physical theatre and devising. He has studied and mastered the techniques of teachers you have only read about. If you never had the good fortune to see the Theatre Jeune Lune, you won't appreciate his genius until you have studied with him.

Information sites and other resources for twin city actors

The Acting Biz by Beth Chaplin

A comprehensive career guide to the TC acting business. Pick it up at **Amazon.com**.

The Minnesota Film and TV organization
www.mnfilmtv.org

An overview of all that is happening in Minnesota as well as links to everything one might need. They also have a casting hotline.

The Minnesota Playlist
http://minnesotaplaylist.com

A wonderfully complete ezine covering everything performance in the cities. Audition and crew call notices for stage and some screen.

The Twin Cities Actor Expo
http://www.twincitiesactorexpo.com

Generally in March. A very inexpensive yearly event featuring classes of all varieties for all levels of actor training, and information about the market. Some are great, some not so great, but as with anything of this sort, you shop around for what you need.

New York City: Broadway, the Big Apple, the heart of American theatre

New York City, the borough of Manhattan specifically, has been a magnet for actors since the beginnings of theatre in the United States. It has been home to thousands of actors, artists, writers, painters, playwrights, dancers, and musicians. For many of us, it is the cultural capital of America. We are drawn to its reputation and its challenge. It has the largest concentration of museums, libraries, symphonies, art galleries, and theatres in the US, and the quality of these institutions is second to none in the world. Any actor worth his or her salt must at least make an extended visit to see what is going on! Should you move there? That is another question entirely.

Over the past ten years or so, New York has become a home affordable only by the wealthy. Rents are so high that most artists are unable to live in Manhattan, and now live in the boroughs from Long Island to Queens to Brooklyn. This distance can make a commute into the city as long as two hours by subway. Broadway shows are now cast with as many Hollywood actors as possible to guarantee out of town audiences. At least 70 percent of Broadway shows are musicals, several are solo performance and new scripts are generally transfers from regional theatres. In December 2014, according to the *New York Times*, there were thirty-five musicals either on or opening on Broadway and twenty straight plays. On the plus side, the musicals are still populated primarily with Broadway musical performers, and only a few feature movie and TV stars (probably because it is difficult to fake dancing and singing well and most actors who can't do those things move to Los Angeles or other markets).

Of the straight plays this past December-February, cast lists included Jake Gyllenhaal and Ruth Wilson (*Constellations*), Helen Mirren was set to open in *The Audience*, a transfer from England, Glenn Close and a bevy of film and TV names were in *A Delicate Balance*, Bradley Cooper was doing *The Elephant Man*, and Larry David was to be featured in *A Fish in the Dark*. Hugh Jackman was doing *The River*, Michael Cera, Kieran Culkin, and Tavi Genison were in *This Is Our Youth*, James Earl Jones, Mark Linn-Baker, and Elizabeth Ashley starred in *You Can't Take It With You*. This is not to say that these actors are anything less than stellar, however, they have credits that make them very attractive to producers. The reason for calling this to your attention is to make it clear that because Broadway's audiences are 50 percent tourists, the way producers put butts in the seats is to fill shows with familiar names from television and films.

T.R. Knight of *Grey's Anatomy* fame is a former student of mine. Several years ago, before he joined the cast of *Grey's*, we had dinner together in New York. He had just finished appearing in a play, *Scattergood*, off-Broadway for which he had received a Drama Desk Nomination. He was excited about the nomination, but as we walked to the restaurant, T.R. spoke of his inability to break through to the best roles and salaries on Broadway. He said that he was going to have to take a role on TV in order to actually "make it" in New York. It was not something he actually wanted to do. This was despite the fact that he had been working non-stop in the city, both on Broadway and off, in addition to appearing in the top regional theatres in the country. As we know, he did take the job, and was never all that happy. He is now back in New York, and is a "name", but the cost was very high.

If we look clear-sightedly at the Broadway stage, we can also see that it is usually populated with at least three transfers from England, and two from Chicago or elsewhere. Additionally, the "solo performance" is currently in vogue, and there are always some novelty shows with acrobats or magicians or other such offerings taking up the limited theatre spaces on the Great White Way. Looked at this way, the chances of appearing on Broadway for a non-musical performer are very low, especially since cast sizes in plays are now kept to a minimum in order to be produced. The situation off Broadway is pretty much the same, the difference between off B'dway and on B'dway consists merely of the differences in location, pay scale, and size of house. Add to that the brief length of time any straight show stays open, and you can pretty well predict that the chances of making a living, on and off Broadway, are slim. The small theatre companies/collectives off-off B'dway are finding it harder and harder to stay alive in Manhattan, being squeezed for rent, and few can pay anything to their artists.

Perhaps a scouting mission to New York would be your best bet, maybe for a month or two. If you are determined to move to New York, you need to be financially, emotionally, and spiritually prepared. You should have your AEA card and/or your SAG/AFTRA as well. New York is too expensive and "actor-overloaded" for you to spend the years necessary there to become a union member. Why would the unions accept more members when so many members are out of work in New York? And, if you don't have an Equity card, auditioning for most shows is not an option. Even where you have a card, you may have to wait for hours, which means taking time off work, to get an audition. The situation for film and TV is a bit less restrictive, because commercials are plentiful and always seeking new faces. I will do a brief overview of those markets later in this section.

Subletting is a great way to discover a neighborhood, and to stay for a short time. Far cheaper than hotels and better than your friend's lumpy sofa! In order to find a sublet your best bet may be to check out Craig's List, **www.craigslist.com**. Also, whether you are a member or not, you are welcome to visit the offices and use the boards at the SAG/AFTRA offices at 1900 Broadway, (212) 944 1030, or the AEA offices, 165 West 46th Street, (212) 869 8530, where actors going on the road often post sublet notices. The Drama

Bookshop, a wonderful resource for actors, is located at 20 W. 40th Street #1, NYC, 10018, (212) 944 0595 and has an announcement board where you can find sublets as well.

A recent report on long-term rental prices in NYC shows the very expensive rates considered normal in the city. And, landlords often ask for two months rent up front and may also seek a security deposit. They will in most cases do a credit report check on you and require two or three credit cards to ensure you are solvent. So, subletting while you decide what to do and where to go is a great way to "break into" the market.

Rental prices in Manhattan are shown below with figures from *The Manhattan Rental Report*, published by the Brooklyn Rental Market Report, **www.mns.com/manhattan_rental_market_report**.

Manhattan rental averages

Non-doorman buildings (average prices)

	Most expensive	Least expensive
Studios	TriBeCa $3,700	Harlem $1,764
One-bedroom	TriBeCa $6,477	Harlem $2,074
Two-bedrooms	TriBeCa $7,020	Harlem $2,727

Doorman buildings (average prices)

	Most expensive	Least expensive
Studios	Lower East Side $3,676	East Village $2,563
One-bedroom	SoHo $6,051	Harlem $3,180
Two-bedrooms	SoHo $8,210	East Village $4,053

The website service which posts these figures monthly is a good place to discover neighborhoods where you might find something a bit less expensive.

Don't forget that you will need to buy a monthly Metro Card (subway and bus) to get around, which costs, $112 per month. A health club will set you back about $96 per month, internet $51.00 monthly, a cappuccino is about $4.50, and a beer will set you back between $5 and $8 depending on your taste for domestic or imported. These figures are from the Numbeo website, **www. numbeo.com**, and are agreed upon by numerous other databases. The figures don't include such actor expenses as going to see shows, acting classes, coaching, or pictures, and résumés. However you look at it, New York is a very expensive place to live in the United States.

According to Equity, approximately 12 percent of its New York members worked as actors either in or out of New York in 2013. This doesn't say how much these actors made in these jobs, it simply refers to the fact that they worked. Of course with SAG/AFTRA wages figured in, I expect that more than 12 percent of NYC actors found employment as performers.

What I am trying to say is that the risk/benefit ratio of living in New York is not in an actor's favor. The cost of living is so much higher than the possibility of making even a modest living that you need to think long and hard about your reason for moving to New York.

If you are set on becoming a New York actor, it is of major importance that you have a union card already in your pocket. Do not believe that a résumé filled with only school shows and non-union work will get you through a door to an audition. While such a résumé will reveal to an agent or a casting director that you are serious about having a career, unless you are stunningly gorgeous they won't take the time to see you without far more stamps in your book. The lines formed at open calls by unrepresented actors are long and arduous. If you have your union cards and a decent résumé, it is possible that you might get an agent or the attention of a casting director. The best way to go to New York is with an introduction from an agent or casting director from your home market, or, even better, going there with a show that has transferred to B'dway. Another approach is to be associated with a director or a playwright with whom you have worked elsewhere.

Even when you do get agency representation, until you are more seasoned as a performer and can be absolutely counted on to deliver at every audition, the agent will remain conservative in sending you out for the jobs and interviews you may most desire to be seen for. Of course, even without a union card, any agent who takes you on will send you out for non-union jobs. You will have commercial auditions if you are anywhere near the fashion of casting in a given year or season. Commercial casting is a numbers game, and every now and then your number may come up. Without your SAG/AFTRA card, you need to figure how much it is worth to you to be running around the city all day to do non-union, low-paying commercials. The ratio of audition to booking, even for a fairly successful actor, is rarely more than one job for twelve auditions. I suggest that you do the non-union circuit for a while and then confer with your agent about it. You need to become used to the way "things are done" and then ask if you can be sent only on commercial auditions with the possibility of getting your SAG/AFTRA card attached. When you are cast in a union commercial, the money is great and in some instances better than film and TV. Currently, there is a lot of confusion concerning fees for actors in any of the new media—i.e. webseries, web commercials, and so forth. Believe me, few people are trying to pay the actors more than a bare minimum. The unions seem to be working on these problems, but be clear that you may be ripped off as a general part of paying your dues.

As in markets other than Los Angeles, most agents deal with film, TV commercials, theatre, and anything else that may pay a commission. Some, however, will do only theatre, or film and theatre but not commercials, or what have you.

Insofar as "bests" are concerned, there are many books written about "Making It in NYC," and many photographers, coaches, classes, and agents listed in them, as well as all the advice you might want about becoming a performer in NYC. The best of those books are listed below. I caution you to make sure that any book you use has been written in the past ten years, especially those concerning moving and living in NYC. The city changes rapidly and books become old quickly!

Where to get your books: The Drama Book Shop in NYC is a store just for actors. It is one of the few remaining private booksellers and is a treasure for all performers. In addition to selling plays, books, CDs, and videos, the shop sponsors seminars, play readings, performances, and whatever else may help actors. The staff are extremely knowledgeable about the books and what is going on generally. If they don't know, it may not be worth knowing! I have called them with only a vague remembrance of a play's title and no recollection of who wrote it, and with only a little bit of work they have found the script and sent it to me overnight.

And of course, there is always Amazon.

Living in the city

Broke-Ass Stuart's Guide to Living Cheaply in New York, 2008, by Broke-Ass Stuart.

Newcomer's Handbook for Moving to and Living in New York City: Including Manhattan, Brooklyn, Queens, The Bronx, Staten Island, and Northern New Jersey, 2009, by Stewart Lee Allen.

The Cheap Bastard's Guide to New York City, 4th edn, 2008, by Rob Grader.

The real, real facts

Starting Your Career as an Actor by Jason Pugatch, an actor and an analytical-type realist is the single most "tell it like it is" piece of writing about the business in New York that I have read. I think it is essential reading for anyone wanting to work in the Big Apple.

Marketing and representation

K. Callan's books are really the best and most concise guides to marketing and representation as well as other sage advice. Buy and read all of them if you can, and if not, these two should suffice:

How to Sell Yourself as an Actor: from New York to Los Angeles (and everywhere in between!), 2008, by K. Callan.

The New York Agent Book: How to Get the Agent You Need for the Career You Want, 2012, by K. Callan.

As with anything, there are other wonderful books on the subject. I recommend the following:

An Actor's Guide—Making It in New York City, 2011, 2nd edn, 2011, by Glenn Alterman.

Acting: Make It Your Business: How to Avoid Mistakes and Achieve Success As A Working Actor, 2008, by Paul Russell.

Just for personal insights from folks who have been around
The Untold Stories of Broadway, 2013, by Jennifer Ashley Tepper, Kindle edition.

For musical theatre folks
Making It on Broadway: Actors' Tales of Climbing to the Top, 2004, by David Wienir and Jodie Langel.

Other resources

www.backstage.com
Huge compilation of information for actors, more lists and articles than you could ever imagine. Including for the first time, the "Call Sheet" featuring the names and contact info for agents and casting directors in the business.

swww.castingsociety.com
Casting Society of America website. Lots of information about who casting people are and what they do. Great articles about various casting directors and casting awards.

www.IMBDPro.com
All about actors, agents, casting directors, films, crews, and who did what, when and where.

www.ibdb.com
The Broadway internet database, sponsored by the Theatre Development Fund and New York State. This terrific website is a searchable database concerning everything that has happened or will happen on Broadway.

www.actorsaccess.com
A site to post pictures and résumés for free, used frequently by agents and casting people, with a listing of jobs by city, most of them non-union. Still, a place to check out. Actors access

is connected to Breakdown Services and Showfax, all of which list jobs on offer. Showfax charges a fee to download sides and breakdowns. Currently a one-year subscription to "The Showfax Advantage" is $68.00 which allows you not only to download the original sides, but be notified of changes as they occur. It also allows you to submit directly to casting directors.

The Drama Bookshop, 20 W. 40th Street #1, NYC, 10018 (212) 944 0595

New York Times Sunday Arts Section

Time Out Magazine, New York

Studying in the city

There are many, many thousands of acting teachers in New York, and as with anything, there are the good, the bad, and the ugly. Be careful of schools that promise you stardom. Many fall for these places because they believe that there must be an easier way than actually studying. Generally, there isn't. A few great schools and teachers (not full time programs) are listed below.

www.hbstudio.org
The Herbert Bergof Studio is the school founded by Herbert Bergof and Uta Hagen in 1945. The Studio, a non-profit organization, is dedicated to helping actors to be more than they believe they can be. The classes are intense and inexpensive. While both Uta and Herbert are deceased, their mission lives on, vested in their excellent teachers. These teachers include such amazing actors as Reed Birney, Laura Esterman, Austin Pendelton, George Bartenieff, and Amy Wright among others. If you visit their webpage, you can see their faculty, their classes, and the prices for them. You can't go wrong at HB.

www.LarrySingerstudios.com
Larry Singer is an acting teacher who meets you where you are in your training and moves you ahead with an enormous wealth of

knowledge to assist an actor's progress. Kristin Linklater of voice training fame, says, "Larry's presence in a studio is encouraging, demanding, enthusiastic and (importantly) he has a sense of humor."

www.barrowgroup.org

The Barrow Group is a theatre school and an acting company offering a wide variety of classes from voice and movement to audition techniques in all media. They are serious about their teaching and demanding of their actors.

www.actingstudio.com

The Acting Studio is strongly dedicated to the work first done by Sanford Meisner. The Meisner technique is one that every actor should have in his or her toolbox. The school, which has ties to the Chelsea Repertory Theatre, features classes in on-camera, monologues, Shakespeare, voice, movement, combat, and even dialect reduction. Acting studio faculty work with great passion and love for the art and their students. They include a list of well-known New York stage directors, film directors, and actors.

Larrymoss.org

Larry Moss has taught at Julliard, Circle in the Square, he has directed all over the world. He has won the Obie, the Drama Desk Award, and many others. He has been an acting coach on films such as *As Good As it Gets*, *The Green Mile*, *Seabiscuit*, and *Boys Don't Cry*. To get to know if you want to study with Larry (if he will accept you), read his acting book, *The Intent to Live*. Larry is a very intense and serious teacher with a great sense of humor. He travels a lot, teaching all over the world, so if you can find him in New York, sign up!

Los Angeles: Hollywood, the Big Orange, Tinseltown

Most of the actors in America grew up watching movies and TV shows. We did not grow up attending theatre, and when we did, in all likelihood, we were taken by our loving parents to see the latest roadshow of a Broadway musical. In high school, most of us did imitations of these same Broadway musicals and realized that the kind of love and camaraderie generated by doing so was greater than any we had ever experienced. It was better than football and you were much less likely to get hurt.

Those of us who could sing and dance got the leads in our musicals, and if we were really, really good, we secretly believed, "I could be a star on Broadway!" However, for most of us carrying a tune and tap-dancing didn't come easily. A new idea was born—we would show them all: we would become movie stars! After all, movie stars didn't have to do much beside say some lines and look fabulous. Our teenage angst was poured into watching the suffering of the beautiful actors up there on the screen and we loved them. We knew that love was at the bottom of it all. Some of us figured another thing out early. We would never look that fabulous, or be that fascinating. So we decided that serious acting was the thing for us: whether film or stage, we knew we had talent because we suffered.

Most of us trundled off to train somehow, whether we went to Miss Debbie's School of Dance, or took singing lessons with Mr. Vern, or decided to learn by doing at the local community theatre, we prepared ourselves. I myself stole money off my father's dresser while he slept to be able to go to dancing class. We went to these places because they were the beginning of becoming something wonderful. As the song says, "Everything was beautiful at the ballet."

And then, something happened. We began to see that there may be something even more amazing about all of it than we had originally realized. It was as if the theatre and its trappings got bigger somehow. Acting became more than showing off, or being a good mimic, or getting applause, or getting the girls, or pleasing the best teacher you ever met. Acting became a calling as much as if we had decided to become priests. In some ways, many of us took vows, vows of poverty, vows of commitment to a thing far larger than we were. We longed for total and absolute truth. Some of us decided to go to conservatories, some to liberal arts colleges with theatre degrees, some went directly to New York or Los Angeles and trained with whoever seemed most likely to feed our addiction. We spent our days and our evenings at it, amounts of time far beyond those of our more practical school mates, because we were in love. These are the people I am talking to. I call us "citizens of the theatre": whether film or TV or stage, we are in the tribe.

For many of us, acting is an addiction, a need to be filled regardless of the cost. We hardy few are the survivors, the people who stuck with it. While our high school friends did normal things like getting jobs, getting married, having children, and buying houses, we postponed all of that in the hopes of playing in the big game, and we decided to move to NYC or LA and sacrifice everything for "a chance to dance."

Los Angeles seems to promise the best fix the world could ever provide. It is where the best pictures are made and where the greatest talents in the world live. For many of us, the desire to join those happy few is too great to resist. The costs are high. Whether we train as actors or not, once we arrive in Sunnyland, we realize what is actually important—beauty. Even when we know that we are "not what they are looking for right now," many of us forget all about acting and art: we get our noses fixed, we lose weight, we lift weights, we dye our hair, we get stuff pumped into our breasts, we do all of these things for a chance to play on the stars' playground.

Most of the actors who do all of this simply end up being very good-looking waiters and cynical readers of the Hollywood trade papers who have lost their souls along with their noses. Why? For the simple reason that Los Angeles is about the easy sell and easy money. How hard is it to see that a woman with a face like a goddess and a body like Barbie's will sell some tickets? And it is obvious that men who look like George Clooney make women shell out lots of bucks to drool over them whenever they decide to appear. Does this say anything about the talent of such beautiful people as Mr Clooney, Natalie Portman, Hallie Berry, Chris Pine, Jake Gyllenhall? No, they are truly talented individuals who also happened, through some quirk of genetics, to be attractive to the world. They are the triple threats: brains, beauty, and talent.

The effect of a movie on an audience is unlike the theatre because film is manufactured, shaped, tweezed, and edited to catch the hearts and souls of its viewers. We sit before a screen twice the size of many of our bedrooms and are hypnotized by the orchestration of sound, color, movement, and beauty that overcomes us in the dark. Actors in such a situation simply need to stay out of the way while the audience does the acting for them in their imaginations. The reason for the "less is more" theory has to do with the viewer's desire to fill the vessel of the actor they most admire. They are not all that interested in interesting choices.

When Los Angeles directors and producers say that they don't like "stage actors," what they are really saying is that they don't want anyone to get in the way of the spell cast by the film. Rightly so—film is a dream experience; theatre is a social and political one. Film viewing is a one-on-one experience. As soon as the popcorn is half eaten, the filmgoer is alone with their experience and no longer a member of an audience. If the actors don't get out of the way of her fantasy, the film fails.

It is a truth that acting is acting wherever and however it is done. One of the many definitions of acting is "living privately in public." Whether the play is a big-time musical, a piece of Pinter, or a social call to action, actors still need to appear to be living in a particular place and time and to be human. The difference between theatre and film has to do with the point of viewing and editing. In the theatre, the actor leads the audience's view; in film, the editor does that. In the theatre, the audience is at a remove from an actor who appears at a distance and therefore smaller. In film, the actor overwhelms the viewer who has few places in which to hide. The cinema is a director's medium; actors are not in charge. Actors don't decide what take makes it into the product and actors don't decide who gets the close-ups. The actor's life in film may be highly rewarded, and he or she may eventually gain some power over their own artistic lives, but most don't.

I had never believed that stars were anything special until I met some. Whether they crawl out of the womb like that, I couldn't say, but I do know that as a casting director I encountered actors who were plainly stars. It wasn't always obvious beauty, but there was always something so engaging, so sexy about them as people, that one couldn't turn one's eyes away. Even these folks needed breaks to make it. The old adage, "if you are good, you will make it," is not true. Perhaps it is better to say, "if you are a potential star, you may get more chances to prove it."

So, I expect that now you are saying, well, that is definitely not me, I'd best get a real estate license. However, as an addict, that may not be so easy. Let me comfort you. In any film, there need only be two or three of these enchanting creatures, and the rest of the actors are regular folks, like you and me! If you recall your high school musical theatre experiences, it was the performing and the camaraderie that you craved, more than the stardom. I mean, it is nice to be the lead, but being the best friend, or the maid, or the killer is just as much fun. Maybe it's more fun because you don't have to carry the entire plot line on your own frail shoulders and you are allowed a bit more creativity.

If you can imagine yourself as one of the hardworking thousands of actors in Los Angeles who don't turn heads and never have to worry about getting a contingency of security guards and lawyers, you might be able to get your fix.

I have not discussed television so far, but in many ways acting on television is far more like stage than film. Television performers are more apt to be like ourselves, not overly gorgeous, not mysterious, and not particularly quirky. They are people we could easily have dinner with. Television actors seem to have a longer career life, we don't mind seeing them every week regardless of the role they are doing. As far as finances, in the long run, they may exceed the earnings of the movie star of the week because they will be around so much longer.

The reality of the business is that it will tell you rather quickly what media you best serve. The agents, the managers, the casting directors, and the directors will pigeonhole you whether you agree or not. Once a TV actor, it is difficult to move to film. Movie actors see TV as a demotion (although that is changing with the advent of independently produced, quality TV). And we haven't even discussed the world of commercials, where the money is great and the respect is not.

Of course, I am putting the cart before the pony here—you haven't even established a foothold in the business, you don't have an agent, no one knows your name, you have never been in a real film, and you live in Pennsylvania. You will need to get some money and go if that is what you really want.

How much money? According to **Rentjungle.com**, as of December 2014, average apartment rent within ten miles of Los Angeles is $2,068. One-bedroom apartments in Los Angeles rent for $1,769 a month on average and two-bedroom apartments rents average $2,377. Most landlords, knowing how actors are, require "first and last" month's rent, plus a security deposit. Go to **http://www. tenant.net** to see the rules governing the responsibilities of tenants and landlords.

Average rental prices in Los Angeles are not the highest in the nation according to a USC study. This study also concluded that rent generally accounted for more than 43 percent of the renter's income, and it is not getting better. According to the Los Angeles Department of City Planning Housing Needs Assessment, the city needs to produce roughly 5,300 units per year that are affordable to moderate-income households or below (Los Angeles Department of City Planning, 2013). Los Angeles has instead averaged roughly 1,100 units per year since 2006. Since 2000, 143,000 rental units that had been affordable to those making less than $44,000 a year have become unaffordable.

Of course, as with most things these days, high rent houses and apartments are plentiful, so if you bring a bucket of money, you won't have a problem. For most of you, though, roommates are a fact of life. Don't forget, you will need a car, car insurance, some inevitable car repair, a place to put the car, and gas. That will set you back between $4,000 and $6,000 per year conservatively. You might want to use Uber or Lyft or other such services that in the short view seem expensive, but in the long view may actually be not only cheaper, but also more likely to help your expense register when tax time rolls around.

Acting classes will cost between $120–300 per month. If you are not in a class, you will have no room to fail except audition rooms and will have few artistic colleagues outside of those people with whom you went to college. Coaches for auditions will average $100 per session and they are often necessary. Health clubs will cost $30–100 monthly unless you simply work out on the beach or with a video in your home gym. Frank Harts, currently appearing in the TV series *The Leftovers*, and a Julliard graduate who did both TV and Broadway before moving to Los Angeles, says:

I would say the two problems I had when I first began were, first, not having a healthy respect for the "business" of acting and thinking that talent alone would allow me to meet my industry goals. And second, I had no understanding of the power of the gym and healthy nutritional regimens, to help one increase the odds of "success."

Grooming will be more expensive in LA, because you have to look your best all the time to stay in the business. According to *US News and World Report*, the average haircut for a man in Los Angeles is $40 and for a woman $69. And that doesn't include color or highlights or brow waxing!

While food prices continue to rise everywhere, food is one item where you will probably not have sticker shock. There are a plethora of fresh fruits and vegetables available for minimal cost, and you may find that you actually have an avocado tree in your yard. The cost of shoes and clothing is equivalent to other markets except that you will not need a winter wardrobe, just more flip-flops!

I have already discussed the price of pictures, mailings, and website design; they are generally consistent with most other large markets. (A word to the wise— don't have your pictures done before you get to LA, and then proceed carefully.) Your entry into the business needs to look professional, but don't blow thousands of dollars on pictures until you and the market negotiate how you are going to package yourself.

In Los Angeles, more than any other market in the world, you must create a specific brand and package. You need to determine, once you have settled into Lala Land, how the industry wants to use you. You must then decide if that is all right with you. If it isn't, change your look, your pictures, your résumés, take a new class, and talk to your agent if you have gotten one by this time. Chances are you will have gotten a commercial agent, but the elusive theatrical agent may still be a few years in your future.

Commercials are the way many working actors pay the bills either fully or partially. There is no dishonor in doing commercials if you do them honorably. You are still representing humans to humans; if you are politically or socially or spiritually opposed to something in a particular spot, don't do it. Don't play a bimbo or a stupid jock unless you want to represent those views in the world. If you are asked to become a character such as Flo in the Progressive Insurance spots, be aware that you will be unable to do anything else until the viewing audience forgets about you. You will become very rich, but artistically you may feel sad. Flo, the Progressive lady, an actress named Stephanie Courtney, made a choice. She is a very funny, quirky, talented, cute, and well-trained actor from NYC who moved into stand-up years ago where she found her niche. It seems to me that once Progressive moves on, she will be able to move back to stand-up and command big money, but she is fairly hemmed in in terms of what kinds of material she will be able to do, and what kinds of roles may be offered to her for the next ten years or so. One of my students was the Sprint Wireless Man and he was perfectly happy with his choice. He had never had ambitions to do more than sitcoms, so the choice was right for him. Those spots are now far in the past, and he will probably begin to do those sitcoms unless he has gotten rusty sitting around the pool.

Ways careers proceed in LA

1   You might first get a commercial agent, it is a business of numbers for them and new faces are usually welcome.

2   You may spend a few years doing commercials, taking classes, getting your finances together, and doing showcases and live shows (yes, those exist in LA).

3   After about four years, you should hopefully be on the verge of getting a theatrical agent and maybe a manager. You should be appearing in episodic TV, sitcoms, or dramatic series. You should have contacts with some casting people, and a community of actors who support each other.

4   By year five or six, you should have both a commercial and a theatrical agent, have done some small roles in films, guest-starred on TV, and be well known within the industry.

5   After that, somewhere between years seven and ten (if you are lucky) you may get a full TV series, or some well-reviewed movies, and you may begin to be noticed by the country at large.

6 After that, you will be on your own and there is no way to predict what will happen.

The most obvious thing anyone can say about LA is that it is constantly changing and long-term success is rarely guaranteed. The casting person who loved you yesterday may be fired, your agent may have a heart attack, your type will change, your manager may drop you, you may be too expensive to hire and too proud to take less, you may have locked yourself into some bad career choices, or you may simply go out of style. It happens to the best of them! My friend, a voluptuous, extremely pretty comic actress, Loni Anderson, was at one time a household name for her work on *WKRP in Cincinnati*. She barely needed a last name. Once the show went off the air, she made some bad artistic choices, had some messy personal problems, and dropped out of the public's imagination. She is still funny and smart, but completely out of style.

I am tempted to say that 90 percent of the actors who are successful in Los Angeles will have the same experience in one way or another. Hollywood eats people, and moves on. If you are going to LA, watch this trajectory and learn from it. If you accept it as a fact of life, you may be able to reinvent yourself just before it happens. If you are a woman, I know I shouldn't say this, but your chances are doubly hard if your career has been built on beauty. Why do you think the former stars and starlets are having the disfiguring plastic surgery? Because they can't let go of their glamorous identities and play the mothers and older women for which they are more suited in the eyes of Los Angeles executives.

So, your career will probably be time-delimited, especially if you are a woman. And it will take far longer than you can imagine. You will need patience, determination, and an exit strategy to keep you sane. This doesn't mean that you shouldn't try. As with New York, I think actors need to feel what it is like to work in LA, but they should do it wisely. Stars in your eyes are blinding.

Below is a list of resources that I believe are most valuable to newcomers.

Bookstores

Skylight Bookstore-
818 N. Vermont Ave., LA, CA 90027
(323) 660 1175
www.skylightbooks.com

A general bookstore with lots of books for actors and performers. This new store features authors, generally from showbiz, reading from their books. It is a real treat and a welcoming space. If you become a member, you get lots of savings. There are also quite a few specialized book club groups that meet at the venue.

Samuel French Bookstore
7623 Sunset Boulevard, LA, CA 90046
(866) 598 8449
www.samuelfrench.com/bookstore

The place to go for scripts, books, t-shirts, and all things LA. A Los Angeles institution! Go to their Facebook page, lots of announcements about goings-on and freebies!

Great advice and information

The Actors Network
www.actors-network.com

A network of working actors sharing trade publications and resources, job leads, helpful tips and warnings, plus moral support.

Backstage.com
www.backstage.com

The indispensable actor's newspaper. News, casting, submissions, and lots of databases.

Daily Actor
www.dailyactor.com

Excellent, full of resources, articles, and advice for Los Angeles actors. Includes some screenplays and lots of great interviews.

Hollywood Reporter
hollywoodreporter.com

General newspaper site about what's happening in the business.

Deadline Hollywood
http://deadline.com

News and views up to the minute.

LA.Com
www.LA.com

Another source of news and info.

Indispensable books

Acting is Everything, 11th edn, 2006, by Judy Kerr.

How to Become a Casting Director, 2012, by Keith Wolfe.

How to Book Acting Jobs in TV and Film: 2nd edn, and *The Truth About the Acting Industry: Conversations With a Veteran Hollywood Casting Director*, 2012 by Cathy Reinking CSA.

How to Get the Part without Falling Apart, 1999, by Margie Haber.

Hit the Ground Running, 2012, by Carolyn Barry.

Self-Management for Actors: Getting Down to (Show) Business, 4th edn, 2014 by Bonnie Gillespie.

The Actor's Guide to Agents, 2014, Samuel French, updated quarterly.

Legitimate casting websites

Actors Equity Casting Call
http://actorequity.org/castingcall

A national website for AEA members, but open to all to read.

Actor's Access
http://actorsaccess.com

Online casting and submission website that submits your headshot and résumé to projects posted by casting directors.

SAG indie
www.sagindie.com

SAG indie films being cast.

National Casting Network LA
http://home.lacasting.com

Website similar to Actor's Access, submissions and casting information as well as other info. Some agents use Casting Networks and some use Actor's Access, it depends.

Now Casting
www.nowcasting.com

Online casting and submission website that submits your headshot and résumé to projects posted by casting directors.

Talent agents

There are so many types and sizes of talent agencies, each of which specializes in different things, that I am not going to list them all.

They can be found listed on any of the websites above and there are new books published every year covering them. The same can be said for photographers.

Support groups for the biz

When you are down and out, lonely, and lost, a support group of actors can lift you up and give you a few industry tips as well. I have chosen those below because they aren't connected to acting classes and they seem the least likely to ask you to pay for anything you don't need or want. Be very wary of being coached by actors in these situations. While an actor may give you his or her best advice, her or she may also tell you something that might lead you down the wrong path. Take an acting class for acting, get a support group for support.

Actors Helping Actors
www.meetup.com/Actors-Helping-Actors

The Los Angeles Actor's Hangout
www.meetup.com/Los-Angeles-Actors-Hangout

A brief list of approachable managers (no drop ins or calls)

Most managers work nationally for their clients. Here are a few that I either know, or whose clients I know.

Thruline Entertainment
9250 Wilshire Blvd, Ground Fl.
Beverly Hills, CA 90212
(310) 595 1500
www.thruline.com
info@thrulinela.com

More/Medavoy Management
10203 Santa Monica Blvd Ste 400
Los Angeles, CA 90067
(424) 298 2300

3 Arts Entertainment
9460 Wilshire Blvd, 7th Fl
Beverly Hills, CA 90212
(310) 888 3200
http://3arts.com

DeWalt Management
623 N. Parish Place
Burbank, CA 91506
(818) 562 7051
Suzanne@dewaltmgt.com

Principato-Young Entertainment
9649 Wilshire Blvd.
Beverly Hills, CA 90212
(310) 274 4474

Billy Miller Management
Billy Miller
8322 Ridpath Dr
Los Angeles, CA 90046
(323) 822 0522
billymillermgmt@aol.com

Principal Entertainment LA
(310) 446 1466
www.principalent.net
Marsha McManus, principal/manager
Elizabeth Robinson, principal/manager
Larry Taube, principal/manager
Liz York, manager
Michael Smith, manager
Atil Singh, manager
Jennifer Weinbaum, manager
Katherine Hatton, associate
Jacob Hastad, associate
Matt Birkel, associate

Justice & Ponder
Todd Justice
Rodney Ponder
PO Box 480033
Los Angeles, CA 90048
(323) 850 2344
www.justiceandponder.com

Sanders Armstrong Caserta Management
2120 Colorado Blvd Ste 12
Santa Monica, CA 90404
(310) 315 2100
Jason Kendziera

Priluck Company
1230 Montana Ave
Santa Monica, CA 90403
(310) 394 2911
Jason Priluck

Studio Talent Group
1328 12th St
Santa Monica, CA 90401
(310) 393 8004
www.studiotalentgroup.com
stgactor@gmail.com
Kathryn W. Boole

The Chesapeake Bay Area, DC and Baltimore

You won't get rich acting in Washington, DC. However, you don't have to be a TV or movie star to headline a show, which often seems to be a requirement in New York. We have plenty of theatres to provide opportunities for artistic expression and for beefing up your experience. The theatre community here really feels supportive— including the patrons. Besides, this is a great place to live a sane life.
ED KELTY

There are actors who live, work, and make a living in the Chesapeake Bay area. It features a rich quality of life and the availability of big city offerings, as well as nearby stretches of sea, sand, wetlands, mountains, and valleys, that make the Chesapeake Bay a beautiful place to spend your life. The climate is generally mild with the exception of some blazing hot summers.

Actors have a great deal to choose from in the area. Everything from television shows to documentaries to independent films to features, to commercial work, web work, new media and government industrials. It's not limited. In the summer the Baltimore Playwright's Festival (**www.baltplayfest.org**) features plays written by local writers and produced by theatres from all over the city.

Where to live? If you want to have access to opportunities in both these vital theatre communities, try looking in the smaller towns and villages sprinkled midway between the two. The prices are lower and the lifestyle easier.

According to **rentjungle.com**, the average rent for an apartment within ten miles of Baltimore is $1,210, as of December, 2014, Rents range from $1,024 for one bedroom to $1,215 for two bedroom apartments. DC is considerably more pricey with average rents coming in at $1,918 within a ten-mile radius. Rent for one bedroom apartments in Washington averages $1,732 a month, and a two bedroom apartment comes in at $2,163. The same goes for all of life's other amenities: parking, gyms, food. The list goes on.

Can you live in this area without a car? Getting your bearings in a new city can be overwhelming and you may shrug your shoulders and saddle yourself with car payments, insurance, repairs, gas, etc., to not have to deal with a maze of choices. *USA Today*'s web page (**http://traveltips.usatoday.com/travel-washington-dc-baltimores-inner-harbor-32550.html**) has some very useful travel tips: "Washington, D.C., and Baltimore's Inner Harbor are about 40 miles apart. Many workers commute daily between the two cities." Check out your options for travel from one to the other, Amtrak, bus service, commuter rail and more. Once in the metropolitan area, the two cities are serious about their mass transit. It's cheaper and much easier to watch a video, read or learn lines on a train than being stuck behind a semi on the interstate.

Selected DC information websites

www.theatrework.org
DC sponsored website by the Helen Hayes people which functions as a free place to store videos of your work as well as pictures and résumés.

http://theatrewashington.org
Another website created by the Helen Hayes Awards dedicated to helping actors and the theatres of the capital city, information about what's going on. According to Theatre Washington, there are over ninety professional theatres in DC.

www.DCmetrotheaterarts.com
Most DC auditions are posted at this website.

http://www.lowt.org
The League Of Washington Theatres website has some great links. It sponsors combined auditions every year and most professional theatre companies attend.

www.actorscenter.org
This non-profit, volunteer-run website is a place to go for all sorts of information on casting, classes, shows, workshops, and just general information. It charges $65, but that seems a fair price considering its value. I strongly suggest getting a membership, it's chock full of great stuff.

https://groups.google.com/forum/#!topic/galvanize/ AMNud2_9m1M
The Greater Washington/Baltimore AEA Liaison auditions in Washington, DC. Combined auditions for both DC and Baltimore theatres.

Selected DC Agents

There are many so-called agents and casting directors in the area, and for DC I can only recommend the one listed below. Be on the lookout for scams!

Capital Talent Agency (SAG/AFTRA/AEA franchised)
Michelle Muntifering, Agent
1330 Connecticut Aveue N.W. Ste 271
Washington DC 20036
www.capitaltalentagency.com
Roger Yoerges, CEO
Ralph C. Cooper, Jr., theatrical/commercial/voiceover
J. Fred Shiffman, legit theatre

Headshot/résumé/demo reel by mail. No electronic submissions.

Selected DC classes

Studio Theatre Conservatory
1501 14th Street Northwest
Washington, DC 20005
(202) 332 3300
www.studiotheatre.org

Registration information at the website. All sorts of weekend and
evening workshops as well as a full conservatory. Weekend
workshops are very inexpensive.

The Theatre Lab School of the Dramatic Arts
733 8th Ave NW
Washington DC 20001
(202) 824 0449
www.theatrelab.org

This conservatory-based school boasts a stellar faculty. It offers a
one-year training program as well as classes for professional actors
seeking to keep their skills alive and to learn some new ones.
Classes are inexpensive and have varying schedules. One of their
great teachers is Kim Schraf. You will be lucky if you get into one of
her classes!

The Shakespeare Theatre Company
Hartman Center for the Arts
516 8th St
Washington, DC 20003
(202) 547 3230 (admin. offices)
www.shakespearetheatre.org

A great variety of classes covering both contemporary acting and Shakespeare performance methods. A wonderful faculty. Nancy Robinette, "The Meryl Streep of DC," teaches at STC and would be a treat to study with. Classes reasonably priced and varied in scheduling.

Photographers

Chris Mueller
http://christophermueller.net

Chris, who is an actor and photographer, was very highly recommended by an industry professional. He is hard to get, but according to my source, worth pursuing.

Colin Hovde
1419 3rd St SW
Washington, DC 20024
(202) 491 9205
www.cstanphoto.com/

A director, actor, former agent, and great headshot photographer, Colin is booked a lot, so as with Chris Mueller, get him when you can.

Theatres in the general DC area

Round House Theatre (mixed AEA)
4545 East-West Highway
Bethesda, MD 20814
(240) 644 1099
Roundhousetheatre.org

Email P&R to: **dcrosby@roundhousetheatre.org**. Auditions: season auditions are held every year. Notices posted on **broadwayworld.com**. Separate auditions for their yearly musical.

The Keegan Theatre (mixed AEA)
1742 Church Street, NW
Washington, DC 20036
(703) 892 0202
www.Keegantheatre.Com
Casting contact: Mark A. Rhea

Snail mail P&R to: The Keegan Theatre, P.O. Box 17407, Arlington, VA 22216.
Auditions posted on their website **www.mdtheatreguide.com**.
Email submissions accepted at **casting@keegantheatre.com**.

Arena Stage (mixed AEA)
1101 Sixth Street, SW
Washington, DC 20024
(202) 554 9066 ext. 249
www.arenastage.org
Casting contact: Daniel Priksarnukul

Submit P&R to theatre address. No email submissions.

Theater J at the Center for the Arts (mixed AEA)
Washington DC JCC
1529 Sixteenth St NW
Washington, DC 20036
(202) 518 9400
www.washingtondcjcc.org

Auditions: Equity and non-Equity actors are seen on a show-specific basis. In general, auditions are by invitation only. Snail mail P&R by mail to: Theater J, attn. casting at the theatre's address or email P&R to: **casting@theaterj.org**.

Discovery Theater (non-AEA)
Smithsonian Institution
Washington, DC 20026
(202) 633 8700
discoverytheater.org

Snail mail P&R to: Discovery Theater, attn: casting, Roberta
Gasbarre, PO Box 23293, Washington, DC 20026 or email to:
info@discoverytheater.org.

Folger Shakespeare Library Theatre (AEA)
201 East Capitol Street
Washington, DC 20003
(202) 675 0712
www.folger.edu
Casting contact: Beth Emelson

Auditions posted at broadwayworld.com. Snail mail P&R to casting
at theatre address.

Ford's Theatre (AEA)
511 Tenth Street, NW
Washington, DC 20004
www.Fordstheatre.org
Casting Contact: Mark Ramont

Email P&R to: **auditions@fords.org.** No phone calls.

The Forum Theatre (mixed AEA)
Mailing address
P.O. Box 73265,
Washington, DC 20056-3265
(202) 489 1701

Performance Space
The Silver Spring Black Box Theatre
8641 Colesville Road
Silver Spring, MD
Casting contact: Michael Dove

Email P&R to: **casting@forumtheatredc.org**.

Gala Hispanic Theatre (non-AEA)
P.O. Box 43209 Washington, DC 20010
(202) 234 7174
www.galatheatre.org
Casting contact: Mariana Osorio

Email P&R to: **mariana@galatheatre.org**.

Journeymen Theater Ensemble (mixed AEA)
P.O. Box 213
Washington, DC 20044-0213
(202) 669 7229
www.journeymentheater.org
Casting contact: Deborah Kirby

Email P&R to: **info@journeymentheater.org**.

Olney Theatre Center (mixed AEA)
2001 Olney-Sandy Spring Road
Olney, MD 20832
(301) 924 4485
www.olneytheatre.org

Casts primarily actors based in the Washington, DC/Baltimore
area. Attends the League of Washington Theatres auditions.
Attends the Greater Washington/Baltimore AEA Liaison Auditions
(in Washington, DC). AEA principal auditions in New York City.
E-mail P&R to **casting@olneytheatre.org**, or snail mail to theatre
address.

Studio Theater (AEA)
1501 14th St NW
Washington, DC 20005
(202) 332 3300
www.studiotheatre.org
Casting contact: Serge Seiden

Attends the AEA Liaison auditions. Attends League of Washington Theatre's open auditions. Non-Equity open calls are typically held for each studio second stage production. Snail mail P&R to: Studio Theatre Casting Office, 1501 14th St NW, Washington, DC 20005 or **casting@studiotheatre.org**.

Teatro De La Luna (non-AEA)
4020 Georgia Avenue, NW
Washington, DC 20011
(202) 882 6227
www.teatrodelaluna.org
Spanish speaking theatre
Casting contacts: Nucky Walder, Peter Pereyra

E-mail submissions to: **info@teatrodelaluna.org**. Actors submitting to Teatro de la Luna *must* be fluent in Spanish.

The Shakespeare Theatre Company (AEA)
516 8th Street, SE
Washington, DC 20003
(202) 547 1122
www.shakespearetheatre.org
Casting contact: Merry Alderman

Send P&R to theatre address, no phone calls, no email submissions.

The Washington Stage Guild (AEA)
4018 Argyle Terrace, NW
Washington, DC 20011-5301
(240) 582 0050
www.stageguild.org

Snail mail P&R to: Bill Largess, producing artistic director at theatre address, no email submissions.

Theatre Alliance (mixed AEA)
(Admin) 2020 Shannon Pl SE
Washington, DC
(202) 241 2539
www.theateralliance.com
Casting Contact: Paul Douglas Michnewicz, (202) 399 7993
ext 101

Theater Alliance auditions actors per show. E-mail submissions to:
pdm100@aol.com.

Washington Improv Theater (non-AEA)
916 G Street, NW
Washington, DC 20001
www.washingtonimprovtheater.com
wit@washingtonimprovtheater.com

Contact via email if you wish to be notified when auditions are
scheduled, no phone calls, no email submissions.

Wooly Mammoth (mixed AEA)
641 D Street NW
Washington, DC 20004
(202) 312 5271
www.woolymammoth.net
Casting contact: Brian Smith

Auditions posted on all major websites (Backstage.com,
Broadwayworld.com, etc.) and on theatre website. E-mail P&R to:
casting@woolymammoth.net.

Theatres: Baltimore and DC Outskirts

1st Stage (AEA)
1524 Spring Hill Road
Tysons, VA 22101
(703) 854-1856
www.1ststagetysons.org

Send P&Rs to: casting, 1st Stage, PO Box 9384, McLean, VA 22102 or email **casting@1ststagetysons.org**, auditions posted on theatre website.

Adventure Theatre (mixed AEA)
7300 Macarthur Blvd
Glen Echo. MD 20912
(301) 634 2270
adventuretheatre.org
Casting contact: Michael J. Bobbitt, Artistic Director

Email P&R to: **info@adventuretheatre.org**.

Center Stage (mixed AEA)
700 N. Calvert St.
Baltimore, MD
(410) 332 0033
www.centerstage.org

Submit P&R to: **casting@centerstage.org**.

Chesapeake Shakespeare Company (non AEA)
7 South Calvert Street
Baltimore MD 21202
(410) 244 8571
cheasapeakeshakespeare.com

Auditions for summer season and following winter season are held in January. Email P&R to: **auditions@chesapeakeshakespeare. com**.

Cumberland Theatre (non AEA)
101 North Johnson Street
Cumberland, MD 21502
(301) 759 4990

Send P&R to: casting at theatre address, email videos/links to **Don@cumberlandtheatre.com**.

Everyman Theatre (mixed AEA)
315 W. Fayette Street
Baltimore, MD 21201
(410) 752 2208
http://everymantheatre.org

Auditions for entire season held in late spring.

Kennedy Center Theater For Young Audiences (AEA)
Arts On The Horizon
P.O. Box 7083
Alexandria, VA 22307
(202) 416 8830
Casting contact: Michelle Kozlak
Email P&R to: **kctya@kennedy-center.org**.

Medieval Times (non-AEA)
7000 Arundel Mills Circle
Hanover, MD 21076
1-866-543-9637 for current opportunities
www.medievaltimes.com/baltimore/
mdjobs@medievaltimes.com

Metrostage (AEA)
1201 N. Royal Street
Alexandria, VA 22314
(703) 548 9044
www.metrostage.org
Casting contact: Carolyn Griffin

E-mail P&R to: **info@metrostage.org**. Prefers submissions from AEA and EMC.

Quotidian Theatre Company (non-AEA)
5705 Brewer Hill Circle, #202
Rockville, MD 20852
(301) 816 1023
quotidiantheatre@comcast.net
Casting contact: Jack Sbarbori

Email submissions accepted.

Rep Stage (AEA)
10901 Little Patuxent Parkway
Columbia, MD 21044
(410) 772 4267

Send P&R to theatre address, no email submissions.

Signature Theatre (AEA)
4200 Campbell Avenue
Arlington, VA 22206
(571) 527 1860
www.signature-theatre.org
Casting contact: Michael Baron, associate director

Email P&R to: **intern@signature-theatre.org**, no phone calls.

Synetic Theater (mixed AEA)
and
Classika-Synetic Theater TYA (Theater for Young Audiences)
1800 South Bell Street
Crystal City, VA 22202
(703) 824 8060
www.synetic theater.org

Send P&R to: Admin, 2611 Jefferson Davis Hwy, #103, Arlington, VA 22202. Auditions posted on all major sites for show-specific auditions.

The American Century Theater (some AEA)
P.O. Box 6313,
Arlington, VA 22206
(703) 998.4555
www.americancentury.org
Casting contact: Jack Marshall

Email submissions to: **info@americancentury.org**.

Unexpected Stage Company (non AEA)
Randolph Road Theater
4010 Randolph Road
Silver Spring, MD 20902
(301) 337 8290
www.unexpectedstage.com

Show-specific audition notices on the website and Facebook.

Baltimore classes

Maryland Ensemble Theatre
31 West Patrick Street
Frederick, MD 21701
(301) 694 4744
www.marylandensemble.org

The Maryland Ensemble Theatre offers courses for children and
adults. They are grounded in improv but include scene study and
musical theatre. Twelve-week classes cost between $175 and $250.
Very cheap!

Olney Theatre Center
2001 Olney-Sandy Spring Road
Olney, MD 20832
(301) 924 4485
www.olneytheatre.org

Performance Workshop Theatre
5426 Harford Road
Baltimore, MD 21214
(410) 659 7830
performanceworkshoptheatre.org

The Performance Workshop Theatre offers training, classes and
workshops. The workshops cost between $200 and $275 and last
six weeks. The individual classes are $75 an hour.

Maryland-centric websites: Baltimore/DC including surrounding areas

MD Theatre Guide
www.mdtheatreguide.com

Baltimore Network of Ensemble Theatres
Facebook

Maryland casting directors

Pat Moran and Assoc.
Pat Moran, CSA, Casting Director
Nick Charles, Casting Associate
Scott Philip Goergens, Casting Associate
3500 Boston St. Ste. 425
Baltimore MD 21224
http://www.patmoranandassociates.com/

P&R: one headshot stapled and appropriately cut to size, sent by snail mail. You must send one other electronically to **patmorantalent@ gmail.com**.

Kimberly Skyrme
4313 Sheridan St
University Park, MD 20782
http://kimberlyskyrmecasting.com/

Email all P&Rs to **KimberlySkyrmeCasting@gmail.com**.

Carlyn Davis Casting
Carlyn Davis, Owner, CSA
Lillian Burch, Casting Associate
Suzanne Kang, Casting Associate
124 E Broad St, Unit C2
Falls Church, VA 22046
www.carlyndaviscasting.com

P&R by snail mail only.

Austin, TX: Hippie Haven in the Red Star State! Keep Austin weird!

We hear about the music scene in Austin almost daily, but other arts prosper there as well. The Austin Film Commission is striving to attract production and succeeding. In addition, the Texas Moving Image Industry Incentive Program makes all sorts of work for the industry very attractive. Many of the actors in Austin work a market from Dallas to Houston to New Orleans and back. Agents frequently have offices in both cities.

The Chamber of Commerce (**www.austinchamber.com/austin/ live/quality-of-life.php**) toots the cities horn pretty well. Thanks to its universities, climate and topography it is a city that could well be considered favorably for an actor. Austin has the same hot and dry climate as most of Texas, but its political temperature is much cooler. It is a blue city and likely to remain that way, maybe its because it is so hilly in that neck of the woods. As for the actor's life, in December, 2014, apartment rent within 10 miles of Austin, TX averaged $1,290. One bedroom apartments – $1,094 a month on average and two bedroom apartment rents average $1,375. How to get around? Like most growing metropolitan areas Austin is expanding its mass transit. **capmetro.org/metrorapid** will give you a good idea of the light rail and bus services that may make having a car less necessary.

Austin information websites

The Austin Creative Alliance
6001 Airport Blvd., Ste. 2280-A
Austin, Texas 78752
(512) 470 4505
www.austincreativealliance.org

Unified auditions. "The mission of the Austin Creative Alliance is to advance, connect and advocate for Austin's arts, cultural, and creative communities." "Each year Austin Creative Alliance partners with the University of Texas at Austin's Department of Radio, Television and Film and the Austin Casting Alliance to host an area-wide general audition that can showcase actor talent. This is an important and unparalleled opportunity for actors to have their work seen by major Central Texas producers, directors, casting directors, and agents."

Central Texas Live Theatre
http://ctxlt.com/

This website features not only audition notices, but also reviews, articles, and other theatre links.

Selected Austin agents

Collier Talent Agency
1001 South Capital of Texas Highway
Suite L-200A
Austin, TX 78746
(512) 236 0500
www.colliertalent.com

No phone, no emails, submission info at website.

Acclaim Talent
4420 Stearns Lane
Sunset Valley, TX 78735
(512) 416 9222
Also in New Orleans

No phone, no emails, snail mail to agency. They try to get to the mail within a month but are very busy!

The Atherton Group (Tag Talent)
Austin Studios, Red Building
1901 E. 51St, Box 18
Georgetown, TX 78723
(512) 930 9301
www.tagtalent.com
Also in New Orleans

No phone, no emails, snail mail to agency. They try to get to the mail within a month but are very busy!

Wilhelmina Model and Talent
100 Congress Avenue #2000
Austin, TX 78701
(512) 370 4959
www.wilhelminaaustin.com

The Wilhelmina Agency was at one time simply a modelling agency, but that changed years ago and the franchise expanded to include actors. Granted most of the actors are rather pretty, but whaddya gonna do? There is a form on the website indicating how to submit. It wasn't working when I checked.

Selected Austin casting directors

Burton Casting
5114 Balcones Woods Dr
Ste 307-437
Austin, TX 78759
(512) 201 0474 & (773) 954 8654
www.burtoncasting.com

Beth Sepko
501 North IH-35
Austin, TX 78702
(512) 472 5385
www.bethsepkocasting.com

Austin theatre companies

City Theatre Company (non AEA)
3823 Airport Blvd. Suite D
Austin, Texas 78722
(512) 524 2870
www.citytheatreaustin.org

Auditions: email, **info@citytheatreaustin.org** to schedule an audition. Season posted on website.

Rude Mechanicals (non AEA)
2211 Hidalgo Street
Austin, TX 78702
(512) 476 7833
http://rudemechs.com

Ensemble-based theatre collective which devises its own material. Auditions posted on Facebook page and on theatre webpage.

Austin Playhouse
6001 Airport Blvd.
Austin, TX 78752
www.austinplayhouse.com

Mailing address: P.O. Box 50533, Austin, TX 78763. Auditions: P&R to **info@austinplayhouse.com**. Postings on Facebook page and on **nowplayingaustin.com**.

Salvage Vanguard Theatre (mixed AEA)
2803 E. Manor Rd
Austin, TX 78722
salvagevanguard.org

Unified Austin auditions attendance. Casting notices posted on http://ctxlt.com/ (Central Texas theatre website).

Vortex Repertory Company (mixed AEA)
2307 Manor Road
Austin, TX 78722
http://www.vortexrep.org/
Fantasy, Sci-Fi, alternative musicals, etc.

Casting notices posted on **http://ctxlt.com/** (Central Texas theatre website). Season announced on theatre website.

Hyde Park Theatre (mixed AEA)
511 West 43rd Street
Austin, TX 78751
(512) 479 7529
www.hydeparktheatre.org
A company-based theatre

Philadelphia: the City of Brotherly Love, Ben Franklin's home, the Place with the Cracked Bell

Unfortunately, and perhaps due to its nearness to New York, the once thriving Philadelphia theatre scene has been underfunded but continues to function. It has eroded to the point where there are few jobs available and making a living is difficult. The largest local funding agency, the Pew Trust, has changed it policies, much to the detriment of the Philadelphia community of artists. Well-respected actors, playwrights, and directors are giving up or moving. The artistic director of the renowned Pig Iron Theatre is getting, you guessed it, her real estate license, and the creator of the award-winning and internationally recognized piece of theatre, BANG, is going back to graduate school to become a speech therapist. For a city the size of Philadelphia, it seems a shame that artists can no longer live there for any period of time. There is some film production in town, some commercial and voiceover work, so it might be a place to get your feet wet. It is only two hours from New York, and you can also get to DC and Baltimore where there is more going on, but unless you are a native to the area, I wouldn't advise it.

Of course, that being said, Philadelphia is a wonderful, lively city with great museums, restaurants, and public works. I am sure that small theatres will still be doing interesting work even if there is no money to support them. It is not expensive to live there compared to the larger cities on this list and it has a good public transportation system. If you are going to be in the mid-Atlantic region, you would be better off to be in Baltimore and DC where there seems to be a more vibrant scene for actors. Lets hope that Philly turns it around soon!

Philadelphia casting directors

There seem to be lots of casting directors and agents in the Chesapeake Bay area. However, when looked at more clearly, many of these businesses are illegitimate masquerades for scams of many varieties. I am listing only those agents and casting directors who do not rip actors off. Many Philadelphia actors work in NYC, Pittsburgh, Baltimore, Atlanta, and DC. They are frequently called directly by casting people, and if they are interested in agency representation, they use agents in Atlanta or NYC.

WARNING: the latest scheme in the Chesapeake Bay area is the practice of calling yourself an industry professional when your true profession is website sales. You will be told that you can register for free at a certain database, and then you are asked to pay quite a bit more for the actual use of spurious services. It has been my experience that the smaller the market, the more vicious the criminals, because they appeal to the vanity of people who have no real information about the business. Their special niche is finding parents who believe that their children will be stars.

Before you begin, visit **www.theatrephiladelphia.org** for everything you ever needed to know about acting and actors in Philadelphia.

Philadelphia casting director

Heery Casting
2618-22E Cumberland St
Philadelphia, PA 19125
http://heerycasting.com/
Diane Heery, CSA
Jason Loftus, CSA

See the website for details concerning self submissions. No drop-ins or phone calls.

Philadelphia agents: (SAG/AFTRA franchised)

AMA
93 Old York Road, Ste 1 #515
Jenkintown, PA 19046
www.amatalentagency.com
Actors, models, artists talent agency

Actor submissions: P&R through agency's online talent registration form or snail mail, attention, New Talent Division. Include statistics: hair and eye color, height, weight, clothing size, shoe size, date of birth, and any union affiliations. They reply within four weeks, if not, resubmit.

Reinhard Talent Agency
2021 Arch Street #4
Philadelphia, PA 19103
(215) 567 2000
www.reinhardagency.com/

Snail mail P&R to agency address or email **submissions@ reinhardagency.com**. Also forward any reel, link to work/youtube channel, or voiceover demo. Once received, you should hear within three or four weeks if they are interested.

Classes

The Philadelphia Acting Studio
7141 Germantown Ave,
Philadelphia, PA 19119
(267) 888 6974
PhilaActing@gmail.com

School requires that you audit a class and have an interview prior to being admitted. Class prices very reasonable. My opinion is that this school is legitimate and has great intentions.

Philadelphia theatres

Walnut Street Theatre
825 Walnut Street
Philadelphia, PA 19107
(215) 574 3550
Walnutstreettheatre.org

The Walnut Street Theatre has a large variety of classes to attend. As with any acting school, your experience is based on the teacher you get and the students in your class. It seems that they are mostly interested in musicals and the classics. The Walnut Street Theatre is dedicated to the casting and employment of local Philadelphia-based talent. All auditions are scheduled by appointment only, and begin in Philadelphia first. EPAs are held in both Philadelphia and New York City for the entire season each spring. They also host The Greater Philadelphia Annual Auditions. Non-local talent can be seen for mainstage productions in New York City during the EPA and chorus calls. This information is released on Backstage and the Actor's Equity website throughout the year. All other New York auditions are by agent appointment only. For consideration, forward your headshot, résumé, and cover letter indicating the show/role of interest to: Brian Kurtas, CSA, casting director at the above address. No calls to the theatre or email submissions please.

11th Hour Theatre Company (AEA)
2329 South 3rd Street
Philadelphia, PA 19148
(267) 987 9865
www.11thhourtheatrecompany.org

11th Hour primarily casts local artists from the Philadelphia area. Equity and non-Equity actors are encouraged to submit headshots and résumé, along with a cover letter, for casting consideration. EPAs are held in Philadelphia and EPA notices are posted by AEA. All other auditions are by appointment only. Submit P&R to: **casting@11thhourtheatrecompany.org**. For any questions regarding casting or auditions, call (267) 987 9865 or email.

1812 Productions (AEA)
421 N 7th St
Philadelphia, PA 19123
www.1812 productions.org

Send headshots and résumés to Noah Herman at the above
address or email **noah@1812productions.org**. 1812 attends the
Theatre Alliance of Greater Philadelphia open auditions in June of
each year and has at least one general open call for AEA members.
Refer to the website for further information.

Arden Theatre Company (AEA)
40 N. 2nd St
Philadelphia, PA 19106
(215) 922 8900
http://www.ardentheatre.org

Arden participates in the Greater Philadelphia Annual Auditions. Go
to the website for details on open calls. Arden auditions are held
throughout the year, by invitation only. To be considered for an
upcoming role, please submit your headshot and résumé to: attn:
casting at the theater address.

Broadway Theatre Of Pitman (mixed AEA)
43 S. Broadway
Pitman, NJ 08071
http://www.thebroadwaytheatre.org

To audition for mainstage shows you need a PIN number (OMG!)
that allows you to access the casting website. Contact Broadway at:
boxoffice@broadwaytheatreofpitman.com. Walk-ups are welcome
and will be seen at the end of each hour after those with
appointments have been seen. Audition details for individual shows
are on the website.

Hedgerow Theatre (AEA)
64 Rose Valley Road
Media, PA 19063
(610) 565 4211
www.hedgerowtheatre.org

Go to **broadwayworld.com** or the Hedgerow website for audition information.

InterAct Theatre Company (AEA)
2030 Sansom St
Philadelphia, PA 19103
(215) 568 8077
www.interacttheatre.org

Audition notices are posted on the website.

Media Theatre (AEA)
104 E. State St
Media, PA 19063
(610) 891 0100
www.mediatheatre.org

Send P&R to: Jesse Cline, artistic director, attn. casting at the theatre address.

Montgomery Theater (AEA)
124 N. Main St
Souderton, PA 18964
PO Box 64033
(215) 723 9984
www.montgomerytheater.org

Audition notices are posted on the website.

New City Stage Company (AEA)
2008 Chestnut Street
Philadelphia, PA 19103
(215) 563 7500
www.newcitystage.org

Audition notices are listed on the website.

Theatre Exile (AEA)
1340 South 13th Street
Philadelphia, PA 19147
(215) 218 4022
www.theatreexile.org

Casting is through annual EPA auditions. Equity and EMC members may request an appointment when casting is announced. Send P&R to **submissions@theatreexile.org**.

Wilma Theater (AEA)
265 S. Broad St
Philadelphia, PA 19107
(215) 893 9456
www.wilmatheater.org

Send P&R to **casting@wilmatheater.org**.

Atlanta, GA: Hotlanta! The Big Peach

While it is not on the subject, I was born in Atlanta and spent quite a lot of time there as a child. I am here to tell you that few places are hotter than there. The city of Atlanta sprawls all over the place, with miles and miles of suburbs, some beautiful, mostly very utilitarian places. The city itself boasts charming neighborhoods, trendy shops, and enough universities to keep it a fairly sophisticated place to live.

As with many of the states in the South which boast that they are "right to work" states, making a complete living as an actor takes some doing, but it can be accomplished. Atlanta actors work all over the South, from North Carolina to New Orleans. They travel! While Atlanta has a great public transportation system, the need for a car to access auditions throughout the region can't be ignored. Rents are very affordable, and the general cost of living is lower than most of the other cities where actors congregate.

Because Atlanta is the "Wall Street of the South," and depending on who you talk to, it seems as if it is finally rebounding from the "recession" that hit us all. Jobs seem rather plentiful currently, and it may be a move you want to make.

Most of the theatres in Atlanta attend the unified auditions (see **http://atlantaperforms.biz**). This event is held once a year in the spring, for both Equity and non-Equity performers, and is sponsored by the Atlanta Coalition for the Performing Arts.

Atlanta theatres

7 Stages (Mixed AEA)
1105 Euclid Avenue N.E.
Atlanta, GA 30307
Admin office: (404) 522 0911
www.7stages.org

P&R to: Michael Haverty, associate artistic director at theatre address. Several open call auditions per year. Auditions posted on website, Facebook, and Twitter. Also by appointment.

Actor's Express (mixed AEA)
887 West Marietta Street NW, Suite J-107
Atlanta, GA 30318
www.actorsexpress.com

Sheila Oliver, casting director

No open calls. Snail mail to her at theatre.

Alliance Theater (AEA)
1280 Peachtree St., NE
Atlanta, GA 30309
(404) 733 5000
www.alliancetheatre.org

The Alliance is the BIG KAHUNA in Atlanta, the oldest and most respected theatre institution in the region. Auditions are by unified attendance. P&R submissions: contact casting at theatre address. Invited calls through agents in Atlanta and NYC. Open calls posted on ATML (Atlanta Theatre Mailing List). Alliance audition information line: (404) 733 4622.

Aurora Theatre (Mixed AEA)
128 East Pike Street
P.O. Box 2014
Lawrenceville, Georgia 30046
(678) 226 6222
www.auroratheatre.com

P&R to: **casting@auroratheatre.com**. Show-specific audition notices on theatre website.

Dad's Garage
P.O. Box 5867
Atlanta, GA 31107
(404) 523 3141
www.dadsgarage.com
Improvisational theatre: no home at present

Casting through their own classes and actors trained elsewhere in improvisation.

Georgia Ensemble Theatre (mixed AEA)
Roswell Cultural Arts Center
950 Forrest Street
Roswell, GA 30075
(770) 641 1260
www.get.org

Unified attendance auditions. Open calls chosen from P&R submissions. P&R to Robert J. Farley, P.O. Box 607, Roswell, GA 30077-0607. Auditions posted AEA Hotline, Unified website: **http://atlantaperforms.biz** and on theatre's own website.

Georgia Shakespeare (mixed AEA)
4484 Peachtree Road, NE
Atlanta, GA 30319
(404) 504 1373
www.gashakespeare.org

Questions to Allen O'Reilly, **allen@gashakespeare.org**. Open auditions in Atlanta posted on webpage and other Atlanta theatre sites. Unified website: **http://atlantaperforms.biz** and on theatre's own website.

True Colors Theater
887 W. Marietta St., Suite J-102
Atlanta, GA 30318
(404) 532 1901
www.truecolorstheatre.org
Specifically African American theatre

P&R to Lisa L. Watson, production manager, at theatre address.
Unified attendance.

Horizon Theater Company (mixed AEA)
1083 Austin Avenue NE, Atlanta, GA 30307
(404) 584 7450
www.horizontheatre.com

Email P&R with letter of interest to **casting@horizontheatre.com**
or snail mail to: Casting, PO Box 5376, Atlanta, GA 31107. Unified
attendance, occasional open calls.

The New American Shakespeare Tavern (AEA and apprentices)
499 Peachtree St., N
Atlanta GA 30308
(404) 874 5299
www.shakespeartavern.com
A pub and restaurant employing only Atlanta-based actors

Auditions are posted to Atlanta Journal and Constitution website.
See Atlanta Coalition of Performing Arts (Unified) website for all
audition notices. Mail P&R to casting director at the theatre address.
Because of the way they work, it is advised that you see a show
before submitting.

Out of Hand Theater
880 Glenwood Avenue, Suite F
Atlanta GA 30316
(404) 462 8836
www.outofhandtheater.com
Primarily company-devised work

Auditions: core company of artists that you get into by auditioning to be an associate artist.

Synchronicity Theater
1389 Peachtree St. NE, Suite 350
Atlanta, GA 30309
(404) 974 3291
www.synchrotheatre.com
Primarily women artists working for social change

Check the unified website for upcoming casting as well as the theatre's own website. Auditions by appointment only. Snail mail P&R to Rachel May at the theatre address.

Ansley Park Playhouse
1545 Peachtree Street
Atlanta, GA 30309
(404) 941 7453
www.ansleyparkplayhouse.com
For-profit comedy show has been running for years

Submit P&R through their online form at: **www.ansleyparkplayhouse.com/auditions.html**.

Essential Theatre Company
1414 Foxhall Lane #10
Atlanta, GA
www.essentialtheatre.com
Original scripts by Georgia playwrights

Do not submit P&R. Check the unified website for upcoming casting as well as the theatre's own website.

Top agents: SAG/AFTRA franchised

Atlanta Models & Talent Inc.
3098 Piedmont Rd NE, #102
Atlanta, GA 30305
(404) 261 9627
www.amtagency.com

The Burns Agency
1317 Sugar Loaf Reserve Dr.
Duluth, GA 30097-4054
(404) 303 8995
burnsagency@mindspring.com

No walk-in submissions. All submissions must be sent via email.
Consult their website to see how to submit P&Rs and voiceover
demos.

Jana VanDyke Agency
4461 Bretton Court NW, Suite 500
Acworth, GA 30101
(770) 529 0655
www.jvagency.com

For potential new talent, send (via snail mail) your current résumé
and most recent professional headshot (and if you have a reel,
please include that also) to agency address.

Richard S. Hutchison Management
3071 Arden Rd. N.W.
Atlanta, GA 30305
(404) 261 7824
Voice talent representation only

Submit an MP3 demo of not more than one minute in length.
Include national and local experience. Email to: **rshmanagement@
bellsouth.net**.

J Pervis Talent Agency
949 Image Avenue, Suite C
Atlanta, GA 30318
(404) 688 9700
(818) 237 5760
www.jpervistalent.com

Stewart Talent
500 Bishop Street NW, Suite A-2, Atlanta, GA 30318
(404) 952 2214
stewarttalent.com/Atlanta

Email P&R to: **submissions.atlanta@stewarttalent.com**.

Avery Sisters Entertainment
2047 Gees Mill Rd, Suite 225
Conyers, GA 30013
(800) 986 5133
www.sisterent.com

The People Store
645 Lambert Dr
Atlanta GA 30324
(404) 874 6448
www.peoplestore.net
Also in New Orleans

Aligned Stars Agency
1155 Mt Vernon Hwy Ste 800
Atlanta, GA 30338
(404) 804 6229
www.alignedstars.com

P&Rs can be dropped off at the front desk, Monday to Friday,
8.00 a.m. to 6.00 p.m.

Atlanta casting directors

Annette Stilwell Casting
PO Box 53017
Atlanta, GA 30355
(404) 233 2278
Mostly Commercials
Send P&R reel by snail mail

Atlanta Casting
Cheryl Lubin CSA
Cameron Gutherie
3162 Johnson Ferry Rd., Suite 260-242
Marietta, Georgia 30062
www.atlantacastingdirector.com

Fincannon Casting
Craig Fincannon
Lisa Mae Fincannon
Mark Fincannon
500-D Amsterdam Avenue,
Atlanta, GA 30306
404 370-1999
www.fincannoncasting.com

A great family and great casting directors, really sweet folks.

Chez Group Casting
Shay Bentley-Griffin CSA
2221 Peachtree Rd NE
Suite D, Box 335
Atlanta, GA 30309
(404) 603 8755
info@chezgroup.com

P&R by snail mail

14

Finale

First, I would like to honor my husband, Walter Brody who has been the source of all my self-confidence. Without him, I would never had dared to write this book.

Second, I would like thank Jacob Stanton for his ability to steer me in the right direction and to know what I mean before I do.

Third, I would like to thank the thousands of actors of all ages both students and old hands who have made my life such a happy one.

Finally, I would like to thank the readers of this book for reading it so fully that you actually got to this last chapter.

Final Words:

Remember: Actors are simply people who want to expand who they are. This is not egotism; it is an almost inborn need. It becomes egotism when the desire becomes linked to money and fame.

Ifs

- If it isn't fun, don't do it.

- If your heart isn't in it, you won't be able to last long enough to do it.

- If you decide not to do it, you won't be a loser.

- If you decide to do it, remember it was your decision.

- If you make the decision, work as hard as you can, and grow as much as you can without losing your heart and soul.

- If you find your heart and soul drying up, stop for a bit, nourish yourself, and others. Return when your heart is at peace again.

Shalt nots

- Do not compare yourself to others.

- Do not compete with anyone but yourself.

- Do not see others in the business as simply contacts; make friends, real ones.

- Never stop training.

Blessings

- To be an actor is a way to help humans understand each other and the world.

- To be an actor is to remain forever open, forever searching, forever discontent.

- To be an actor is a journey of investigation into worlds and peoples you would never be able to take in any other life pursuit.

- To be an actor is to be deeply and fully human—if you do it right.

Warnings

- Beware of becoming the center of you own world.

- Beware of the jealousies and angers that can result from the trials, upsets, and poverty that you will undoubtedly encounter.

Index